Dear Sir,

Our meeting in California made a huge
influence on me.

I was extremely impressed by your knowledge
of Polish history.

Please accept this little gift as a reminder
of my stay.

Thank you for unforgettable days.

Hania Carey   24.12.2008.

THE WORLD HERITAGE

POLAND ON THE UNESCO LIST

Bank~BPH

Mecenas Kultury 2006

ADAM BUJAK

THE WORLD HERITAGE
POLAND ON THE UNESCO LIST

2nd edition - complemented

K BIAŁY KRUK

Concept and Design
Leszek Sosnowski

Text by
Krzysztof Czyżewski

Introduction by
Tomasz Orłowski
Secretary General
of the Polish UNESCO Committee
in the years 2001-2004

Editorial assistance and captions
Jolanta Lenard
Krzysztof Czyżewski

English translation
Eunika Bogucka-Jamka
Tomasz Chwaja
Michał Pawica
Piotr Krasnowolski
Language consultant
Anna Wielopolska
Aleksander Ptak

German translation
Jacek Pleśniarowicz
Jolanta Lenard
Language consultant
Medienbörse

French translation
Magdalena Leszczyńska-Benitez
Language consultant
Bernadette Dauban-Lacoste
Marie-Françoise Prat

DTP
Studio Biały Kruk

Printed in the Czech Republic

Cover photo:
The Piast Eagle from the times
of Casimir the Great, over the entryway
to the Royal Wawel Castle.

2nd edition - complemented
Cracow 2007

ISBN 978-83-60292-32-9

*To Jola Sosnowska
for her help and patience
in the time of my illness.*

Adam Bujak

The Goals and Values of the UNESCO World Heritage List

The 1972 Paris Convention concerning the protection of the World Cultural and Natural Heritage UNESCO has so far been ratified by 183 countries. The Paris Convention is one of the most universal normative acts to have ever arisen within the United Nations community. Dynamic development of the UNESCO World Heritage List, established by the Convention, and the rapid increase in inscription applications have resulted in 830 registered sites, from 138 countries around the world.

The World Heritage Convention has without doubt deeply changed our perception of historical sites, their place in society – both on local as well as international levels – and the influence they have on sustained and permanent progress. Inscription onto the World Heritage List is a driving force and a goal for various undertakings of many local communities. The inscription policy cannot, however, be satisfactory to all. Especially, that the nature of the List changed very quickly. Initially, it was supposed to be a sort of restricted catalogue of monuments of art and nature, which would make up a worldwide canon of cultural heritage. Artefacts of human habitat and activity, drawing back on the common history of mankind. For these reasons we can be really proud, that the first inscriptions on the List had already covered two Polish historical sites: the Historic Center of Cracow, and the Wieliczka Salt-Mine.

It is important though to distinguish between the objectives held by the Convention creators from some of the expectations that it evoked. In short, these goals can be focused on two issues: (a) joining elements of natural beauty and human creativity; (b) increasing the society's interest in heritage sites through promoting still higher standards of protection and custody. They establish a very peculiar and original method of perceiving human heritage. This is not the approach typical of natural scientists and art historians. It is a gentle stimulation of sensibility and thoughtfulness of the possibly widest circles of every society. This is also not a nation-oriented approach towards heritage. A site needs to possess universal qualities of global relevance – if it does not, it cannot be registered on the List. We should keep that in mind when looking at the Polish UNESCO sites. Their choice may astonish some, but it allows us to look at ourselves through the eyes of others, and in this way to better understand ourselves. Polish heritage sites on the UNESCO List – continuously updated – illustrate our influence on world civilization.

The goals of the Convention, as outlined above, and the inscription policy can be concisely characterised as heritage seen through the eyes of democratic society. Such society focuses itself around universal values, and preserves them for posterity. This approach strives to set aside the various competing scientific, environmental and conservatorial agendas, in favour of common goals and shared responsibility.

The Convention establishes specific criteria for determining the universal value of the applicants, in order to classify them as sites of World Heritage. For cultural sites there are six (C) selection criteria applicable:
(I) – a site has to represent a masterpiece of human creative genius, or
(II) – it needs to represent important influence on developments in architecture, or (III) – it has to bear a unique or at least exceptional testimony to a cultural tradition, or
(IV) – it has to be an outstanding example illustrating significant stages in human history, or
(V) – it must be an outstanding example of traditional human habitat or land use, and
(VI) – only a site associated with great historic events will be considered.

The natural heritage sites are verified based on the four (N) criteria:
(I) – a site is to be an outstanding example representing a major stage of Earth natural history; or (II) – it has to constitute an outstanding example representing significant on-going ecological and biological processes, or (III) – it needs to contain superlative natural phenomena or areas of exceptional natural beauty and aesthetic importance, and
(IV) – it has to encompass areas of biological diversity, requiring particular conservation.

Based on these criteria, Poland obtained thirteen inscriptions on the List, in total covering 19 accumulated historical sites. The gathering of documentation and argumentation of the universal values of additional sites, are underway. We hope to significantly increase Polish entries on the List. Not only for the prestige of Poland, but also for the benefit of the protection of the various heritage sites, placed in our care on the behalf of past generations, and for posterity.

Here is a short synopsis of the Polish sites on the UNESCO List:

The Historic Centre of Cracow (1978) – Cracow old town, situated at the foot of the Royal Wawel Castle – a symbol of Polish statehood and the site of royal coronations and royal sepulchres. It is distinguished by Europe's largest medieval market square, one of world's oldest university buildings and the Kazimierz district containing many Jewish memorial sites. Criteria: C (IV).

The Wieliczka Salt-Mine (1978) – boasts the rock salt deposits, mined continuously since the thirteenth century. Its 300 kilometres of subterranean galleries and corridors constitute an impressive work of both natural architecture and human hands. It provides a fascinating journey through the history of a major industrial undertaking, changing together with technology and organization of labour. Criteria: C (IV).

The Auschwitz-Birkenau Concentration Camp (1979) – established by the Third Reich, it is the world's largest extermination and slave labour facility. It constitutes of the complex of the concentration camp and the death camp, it bears witness to the Nazi genocide. It is a symbol of human cruelty and, being contrary to all values promoted by the World Heritage Convention, it was placed on the List as an exception. Criteria: C (VI).

The Białowieża National Park and Biosphere Reserve (1979)

– Poland's oldest national park, located in the last remaining stretch of primeval European lowland mixed deciduous forest, rich in fauna and flora. It is the natural habitat of the European bison – species extinct elsewhere on the continent. This area of strict natural reserve was also amended by a similar reserve situated in Byelorussia, making it a transboundary World Heritage site, and facilitating co-operation on nature preservation and biosphere exchange. Criteria: N (III).

The Historic Centre of Warsaw (1980)

– nearly totally ruined by Nazi troops during the Warsaw Uprising, the city was after the war meticulously restored, owing to a remarkable mobilisation effort by the Polish society. The rebuilt objects spanned the time since the thirteenth century. Pinnacle of the reconstruction was the restoration of the Royal Castle – symbol of nation's statehood and survival. The communist governments long forbade the castle's rebuilding. Criteria: C (II, IV)

The Old City of Zamość (1992)

– Polish implementation of the Italian Renaissance conception of the "ideal city". It is a junction of trade routes linking Western and Northern Europe with the Black Sea. Zamość was a multi-national city of many faiths, and a perfect example of the diffusion of Italian and Central European architectural traditions. Its regularity and homogeneity makes it unique amongst other "ideal" urban establishments of this sort. Criteria: C (IV)

The Medieval City of Toruń (1997) – the

town owes its origins to the Teutonic Order. It served the monk-knights as a base for the conquest of Prussia. It quickly developed into an important trade centre – a joint urban arrangement of the Old and New Towns and the castle. Criteria: C (II, IV).

Castle of the Teutonic Order in Malbork (1997) – a monastic castle, substantially

enlarged after the headquarters of the Grand Master was moved there. It is the world's largest medieval brick fortress. Its nineteenth-century restoration is a particularly fine example of conservation techniques. The castle's post-war restoration was made possible due to detailed documentation prepared by earlier conservators. Criteria: C (II, III, IV)

Kalwaria Zebrzydowska (1999)

– a breathtaking cultural phenomenon with the striking beauty of Mannerist architecture strengthened with the power of spiritual experience, stemming from Counter-Reformation thought and folk piety. It is a place of beauty – with harmonious and symbolic representations of the sites of Christ's Passion. It transposes the topography of Jerusalem onto the Polish landscape. The area has remained virtually unchanged since the seventeenth century, and is still the destination of religious pilgrimage. Criteria C: (II, IV).

Churches of Peace in Jawor and Świdnica (2001) – Europe's largest

timber-framed sacral structures. They were erected due to a compromise included in the Peace of Westphalia treaty, which put an end to European religious wars. Built within the framework of specific social circumstances of Lower Silesia, their architectural forms are more akin to Roman Catholic structures than to Lutheran architecture. Criteria: C (III, IV, VI).

Wooden Gothic Churches of Southern Małopolska (2003) – a complex of six

countryside churches. They are a fine example of the adaptation of stone and brick architectural solutions and urban Gothic aesthetics to traditional rural construction carpentry. They represent a particular type of late-medieval aristocratic establishments, resulting from changes in estate administering and awakened desire for family prestige. Criteria: C (III, IV). By Małopolska we mean the former

historic region, and not the current voivodeship. Some of the churches are situated within the boundaries of the new Podkarpackie Voivodeship.

The Muskauer Park (2004) –

a picturesque landscape park created by Prince Hermann von Pückler. It is a cross-border element of the site, as it stretches on both sides of the Lusatian Neisse along the Polish-German border. The park is considered to be the world's first attempt at creative intervention in the natural forest habitat and turning it into a park complex. The park's creation introduced new tendencies in garden design and contributed to the development of landscape architecture in Europe and America. It is Poland's first inscription on the World Heritage List which was motivated by criterion I, that is the recognition as a masterpiece of human creative genius (criteria I and IV).

The People's Hall (The Centennial Hall) in Wrocław (2006) – a monumental

exhibition hall erected at the beginning of the 20th c. to commemorate the centenary of the Battle of Leipzig, as testified to by the structures original name – Centennial Hall. The hall is a great engineering achievement as an innovative application of reinforced concrete construction techniques, and it also continues the tradition of the most magnificent dome constructions in history. At the time of its construction, the dome covering the Hall was the world's greatest work of the kind and it became a model for the entire architectural output of the 20th c. The international critics of the candidature for the World Heritage List underlined that the daring and the modern technological solutions of the People's Hall put it on par with Paris' Eiffel Tower (criteria I, II, IV).

Dr Tomasz Orłowski

Contents

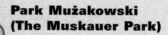

Park Mużakowski
(The Muskauer Park)

Jawor

W

Świdnica

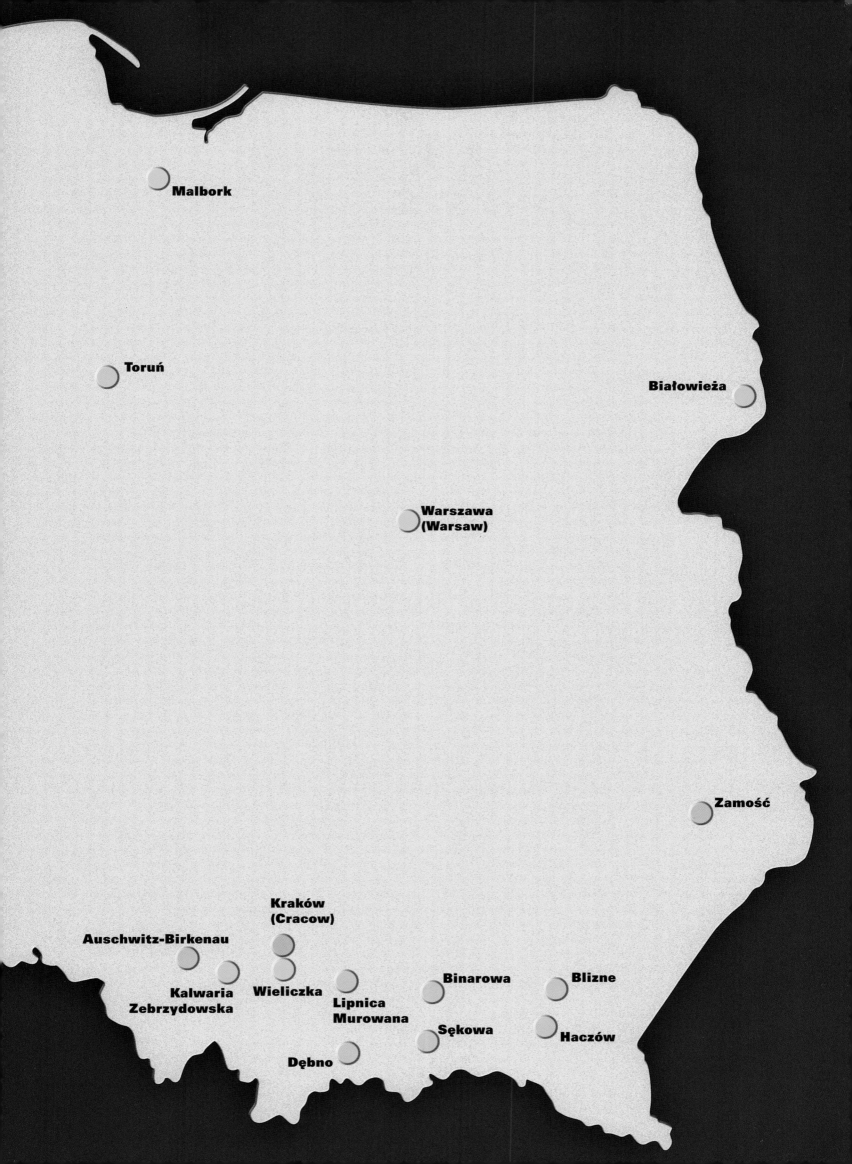

Malbork

Toruń

Białowieża

Warszawa
(Warsaw)

Zamość

Kraków
(Cracow)

Auschwitz-Birkenau

Binarowa

Blizne

Kalwaria
Zebrzydowska

Wieliczka

Lipnica
Murowana

Sękowa

Haczów

Dębno

The exquisite copperplate engraving print of Cracow – over one meter in length – reproduced in the work *Civitates: orbis terrarum*, and published in Köln, in 1617, presents the Polish Crown capital in all its vastness, together with the surrounding towns and suburbs. Its 1619 copy boasts the following inscription: *CRACOVIA TOTIUS POLONIAE URBS CELEBERRIMA ATQUAE AMPLISSIMA REGIA ATQUAE ACADEMIA INSIGNIS*, meaning: *"Cracow, the most famed city in all of Poland, also the most ample, royal and boasting the academy"*.

The Historic Centre of Cracow, entered onto the first World Heritage List in 1978, is still the vibrant centre of a large metropolis, counting nearly a million inhabitants. The town was shaped over a thousand years, with every passing century imprinting its specific mark. Still readable is the grid-work of squares, streets, and buildings, confirming the remarkable spirit in which it was laid out, when Prince Boleslaus the Wry-mouthed issued its foundation charter in 1257. It was then that the great town square (some 200 meters on edge) was staked out, as was the adjoining smaller market square (the current Mały Rynek), and the network of streets crossing at right angles.

Let us now try and take a look at Cracow – a city abounding in Gothic churches, Renaissance palaces and houses – through the eyes of an early-seventeenth century traveller. Back then, it must have evoked admiration of foreign visitors. One of them was the author of a sketch from which the above-mentioned engraving was made. So, let it take us back some four hundred years…

Cracow is surrounded with medieval fortifications. They form a wall of several dozen densely positioned towers, gates, and ramparts. There is also a moat. In the modern times their defensive values gradually decreased, and at the turn of the nineteenth century they became an obsolete burden. During the period of the Cracow Republic (1815-1846), they were torn down to make room for a public park. It was named the Planty Park. The only reminder of the former defensive system is a wall segment, including three towers: the Haberdashers' (Pasamoników), Jointers' (Ciesielska) and Carpenters' (Stolarska) and the most important of the seven city gates – called the St Florian's Gate, as it leads towards the St Florian Church. Just in front of the gate stands the Barbican – a turret-bristled masterpiece of late-medieval military architecture (dating from the late fifteenth century). For hundreds of years it played the role of a formal city gateway. It was through here that kings, victorious commanders, and unfortunately occupants entered the capital.

Two buildings tower over the city. The first is the Town Hall Tower – constructed in the middle of the Town Square, it symbolises the city's independence and autonomous powers. This beautiful Gothic structure blissfully survived to our times, contrary to the town hall itself, which was torn down in the first half of the nineteenth century. The second one is the town's main parish-church – the St Mary Basilica – topped with two uneven towers. The Basilica invokes the Assumption of the Holiest Virgin Mary and was constructed in stages during the fourteenth and fifteenth centuries. There is not enough room here to describe its exquisite furnishings, but let us just mention that the high altar – work of the ingenious sculptor Veit Stoss – is one of the most perfect examples of late-medieval European art. For hundreds of years now, *the hejnał – a bugle call* – is being played from the taller of the two towers. It is fair to say that nearly every Pole knows it by heart.

Much could be said about other churches as well: the collegiate ones, the parish-churches and the monasteries. Not for nothing is Cracow called the second Rome. The churches represent various styles: Romanesque (St Andrew's, St Adalbert's), Gothic (including the Franciscan and Dominican Churches) and Baroque (for example, SS Peter and Paul, St Anne's). They are frequently accompanied by chapels. Among them are family mausoleums – proudly topped with copulas, more modest burgher chapels and ones commissioned by brotherhoods and guilds.

Every town's spirit is defined by its cityscape. The oldest of Cracow's stone and brick structures were constructed as early as the 1300. Their former ground floor rooms are currently used as cellars, because the level of Cracow streets and squares rose significantly already in the fourteenth century. Those fairly modest buildings were gradually replaced by Gothic structures. Many of them were thoroughly transformed during the sixteenth century, when their high raised tops were pulled down and replaced with Renaissance attics. Due to their exquisitely decorated façades, arcaded courtyards and luxurious furnishings, some of them may easily be called palaces. They were inhabited by the most affluent town patricians, representatives of the higher clergy as well as the aristocracy and nobility.

Cracow is towered over by a prominent limestone hill – the Wawel. The hill is densely built up and surrounded with high defensive walls and towers of the royal residence. On the old copperplate, we can see the palace raised on the orders of Sigismund the Old (1467-1548) by the Italian architects: Francesco Fiorentino and Bartolomeo Berecci. The palace is considered to be among the greatest masterpieces of Renaissance Europe. Its awesome interior furnishings were unfortunately destroyed in

Cracow – Metropolis of the Polish Crown

wars and fires, but the impressive courtyard – surrounded with three tiers of galleries, supported by columns – has survived until today.

Next to the palace, there is the Gothic cathedral, dating back to the fourteenth century. It was constructed over the previous, Romanesque structure – built over with Renaissance, Mannerist and Baroque chapels. Its star attraction is the Sigismund Chapel, covered with a gilded dome and justly called *"a pearl of Renaissance, north of the Alps"*. The Cathedral – from 1320 to 1734 the coronation temple of Polish kings – houses the sarcophagi and funeral monuments of Polish royalty and national heroes. This is a true Polish Pantheon. The central location is taken by a very special altar. Here rest the relics St Stanislaus, Poland's main Patron Saint. The Cathedral Treasury houses priceless vessels and canonicals, together with other historic objects, such as the spear of St Maurice – given to the Polish King, Boleslaus the Brave by the German Emperor, Otto III during the famous Gniezno summit in the year 1000. The most important religious and state celebrations, such as Karol Wojtyła being elected Pope in 1978, are accompanied by the stern and rhythmic toll of the great Sigismund Bell, dating from 1521.

The old print also shows the Vistula River, meandering at the foot of the Wawel. It was once a major artery, facilitating the transport of Polish grain and other goods down to Gadńsk, and from there out into the world. Embraced island-like by the river's two arms stands Kazimierz – a city founded in 1335 by Casimir the Great. On the panorama, we recognize the mid-sized tower of the Town Hall, standing on a spacious market square (today Wolnica Square), and also – most importantly – the massive edifices of two Gothic churches: the parish-church of Corpus Christi and the Augustine Monks' church – dedicated to St Catherine. We can also see the small, but clearly visible owing to its location atop a limestone hill, Skałka church. In 1079 it witnessed the martyrdom of St Stanislaus. On the opposite side of Kazimierz is a district, with the Latin name *Oppidum Ludeorum*. This is the densely populated, vibrant and urban Jewish quarter. For many centuries it was governed by its own laws. It was also the centre of high culture and learning, famous among Jews across Europe. Even today, numerous Jewish pilgrims arrive to visit the tomb of the great Rabbi, Isserles Remuh. A sign of religious and cultural diversity of this part of town is the clear outline of the Old Synagogue attic.

From the north, just outside the Cracow fortifications there is a town – for centuries composing the third part of the vast *tripolis*. It is a city of low, medieval houses. Established in 1366, it bears the name Kleparz. It was also often called Florence, after the nearby Church of St Florian.

Finally in the background, on the limestone hills of Krzemionki, there looms an earth mound, erected in honour of the town's legendary founder, Prince Krak. Cracow legends, however, are quite another story. The same goes for the life in the magical city of Cracow...

The old town as seen from Krzemionki district.

The Barbican from 1498-1499, a fragment of the medieval fortifications – the largest preserved fortified structure of this type in Europe.

The Dormition of the Virgin scene in the middle section of the late-Gothic high altar at St Mary Basilica. Veit Stoss's famous work of art.

View from the music choir towards the high altar created by the Master of Nuremberg from 1477-1489, Gothic stained-glass windows from the second half of the 14th century and Jan Matejko's paintings on the walls and ceiling.

◁
Page 14:
Jan Matejko Square with the Grunwald Monument and the Academy of Fine Arts building (on the right). In the background, the characteristic outline of the Barbican and St Florian's Gate and, further off, the towers of St Mary's Basilica and Wawel Cathedral.

The Crucifix from the end of the 15th century carved by Veit Stoss in the side aisle of St Mary's Basilica.

St Florian's Gate, from the turn of the 14th century, is
one of the medieval fortifications remnants.

◁
The brick Gothic Church of the Holy Cross
from the 14th century as seen from the
Planty Park.

St Anne's, the university collegiate church, a Baroque structure constructed in 1689-1703 and designed by Tylman of Gameren. View from the Planty Park.

The Carmelite Church in Piasek, reconstructed in the Baroque style following its destruction during the Swedish Deluge.

The Clock Tower, the highest of Wawel Cathedral towers. The spire featuring the figures of Saints: Stanislaus, Adalbert, Wenceslas and Casimir designed by Kacper Bażanka dates back to 1715-1716.

Page 23:
The 14th century Carpenters' Tower and the adjoining Arsenal building, further off – the Piarist Church.

Constructed under the inspiration of Roman Baroque architecture, the Jesuit Church of SS Peter and Paul (1597-1635).

The western slope of Wawel Hill featuring fortifications from the late 18th century. The visible small turret has, since 1918, served as an entrance to the Dragon's Den.

Wawel pre-Romanesque shrine – Rotunda of the Holiest Virgin Mary (SS Felix and Adauctus) from the turn of the 11th century. A fragment of the Lost Wawel archaeological reserve.

◁
St Leonard's three-aisled Romanesque crypt, part of the former Wawel Cathedral – turn of the 12th century.

The silver coffin of St Stanislaus supported on the shoulders of four angels, crowned by the Saint Prus I coat of arms of and bishops' insignias held by a pair of angels – Peter von der Rennen (1669-1671).

Royal coronations and burials took place in the Wawel Cathedral from the 14th to the 18th centuries and in the 19th and 20th centuries, it became a national Pantheon.

The tomb of Casimir Jagiellon in the Holy Cross Chapel, dating back to 1492, is a masterpiece by Veit Stoss.

The king's head was carved in spotted Salzburg marble.

Triptych of the Holy Trinity dating back to 1467 in the Holy Cross Chapel.

A fragment of the Cathedral's ambulatory with the Gothic tombstone of Casimir the Great and the Baroque monuments of kings: Michał Korybut Wiśniowiecki and John III Sobieski.

The Gothic St Mary's Chapel dating back to the third quarter of the 14th century, with the epitaph of King Stephen Bathory (on the left).

The Renaissance Sigismund Chapel designed by the distinguished Italian architect Bartolomeo Berecci (1519-1533).

The Envoys' Staircase in the eastern wing of the Wawel residence leading to the elegant royal apartments on the second floor.

The fireplace in the Birds' Hall, a remnant of the magnificent castle interior from the reconstruction during the period of Sigismund III Vasa.

The Audience Hall – the historical seat of parliamentary debates, covered with a ceiling featuring sculptures of human heads.

A tapestry featuring Poland's coat of arms of 1560. A gift from
the Horodło starost, Krzysztof Krupski to King Sigismund Augustus.

The Polish Crown's coat of arms
– a fragment of a Wawel tapestry, one of
many pieces weaved in Brussels' workshops
between 1553 and 1571.

A panorama of Cracow with a view of Kazimierz, founded in 1335 by King Casimir the Great.

◁
The inauguration of the academic year in the Collegium Novum hall (1883-1887) of the Jagiellonian University. On the wall there is a portrait of King Casimir the Great, founder of the Cracow Academy (1364), painted by Leopold Löffler.

A panorama of Cracow with a view
of Kazimierz, founded in 1335 by King
Casimir the Great.

Page 40:
The impressive four-level boxes
of the Juliusz Słowacki Theatre, arranged
around the auditorium in a semicircle.
The hall can seat 936 people.

The Old Synagogue on Szeroka Street in Kazimierz – currently a museum of the Jewish culture.

The Remuh Jewish cemetery on Szeroka Street, one of the oldest in Europe, was used as a burial site from the second half of the 16th century until the mid-19th century.

The building was erected in 1891-1893 and designed by architect Jan Zawiejski.

The Juliusz Słowacki Theatre is an eclectic structure modelled on the Grand Opera in Paris.

ot far off from Cracow, there is a little town of Wieliczka. In fact it is one of the city's suburbs. There is the market square, a modest parish-church, a recently restored castle, and a fragment of defensive walls, naturally with a tower. This would be all to little to attract any greater interest. There is, however, another town on the site. It is larger and subterranean, with long corridors, vast chambers, tunnels, and shafts. It is the world famous salt-mine. It is perhaps not a real town, but rather a peculiar, half real and half fantastic magical world, ruled over by the mythical gnome – Skarbek (Treasure Keeper).

It is hard to believe, but salt was once as valuable as gold. The mining rights belonged to the rulers and lucky were the kingdoms that had salt deposits within their boundaries. The Polish Kingdom was amongst them. Poland's well-being and good fortune depended in major part on the income from the Bochnia and Wieliczka salt-mines.

Discovery of the rich Wieliczka salt-mine soon acquired a charming legend. "In 1238, Boleslaus the Chaste, King of Poland was engaged to the Saint Kinga (also known as Kunegund), the daughter of Bela IV. The betrothed princess, not wanting any dowry in gold or silver, asked her father to give her something that could serve the rich and poor alike. Her father consented, and Kunegund set off to a Hungarian salt-mine, into which she dropped her engagement ring. Upon arriving in Cracow, she asked to be taken to Wieliczka and ordered her servants to dig down into the ground. Following her will, they found salt and in the first lump they discovered her engagement ring." In that legend, people kept alive the memory of their saint queen, who as a keeper of the treasure opened the gates to their realm. (J. Mączyński,

Pamiątka z Krakowa, vol. 3, Kraków 1845, pp 283-284). It is important to remember though, that the quoted legend is also claimed by the nearby Bochnia. The Bochnia salt-mine is considered to be older than the one in Wieliczka.

The history of town and mines are tightly interwoven. The proof is in the very name of the town. It derives from Latin *Magnum Sal*, that is *Wielka Sól* (Great Salt). The surface saline springs were already taken advantage of in the mid-Neolithic age. The turning point, however, came in the thirteenth century with the advent of systematic excavation of rock salt. In 1290, the town received a foundation charter issued by Prince Przemysł II. The following two centuries brought development and wealth to Wieliczka. The defensive walls (with 21 towers), the St Clement Parish Church and also the Saline Castle, were all built in those days. Many of the shafts, such as the "Świętosławski", the "Wodnej Góry" and the "Regis" ("Royal"), were all opened back then. The latter was constructed on the request of King Casimir the Great, who also regulated the salt-mining rules by issuing in 1368 the *Porządek górniczy* (The Mining Order).

Until the fall of the First Polish Republic, the income from the Cracow Salt-Mine had been a fundamental part of the state budget. The salt-mine shared the fate of the state. In spite of devastations suffered during the 1655-1657 Swedish Deluge, and subsequent neglect, it came to flourish again. The mine was also affected by natural disasters: fires and floods. Several years ago, both the mine and the town were exposed to a serious bout of flooding. Vast conservation efforts and the planned filling of some chambers and passageways halted the destructive processes for the time being.

The present day salt-mine extends to the depth of 64 to 327 meters, with more than 300

kilometres of tunnels, over nine levels. Industrial scale mining has been already abandoned. Routes available to tourist stretch for over four kilometres, and provide visitors with an awesome view of – unique to Wieliczka – salt figures and reliefs decorating numerous chambers. They had been carved in salt by talented mineworkers, such as Tomasz and Antoni Markowscy, Antoni Wyrodek, and Mieczysław Kluzek. The oldest of the works come from the seventeenth century. Spectacular and unique are the underground chapels – monuments to the miners' piety. The largest of them (50 meters wide and 12 meters high) and at the same time the mine's star attraction is the Saint Kinga Chapel. Apart from the works of art, great interest and admiration is evoked by the impressive system of wooden supports in the chambers and tunnels.

Nature itself works miracles as well. Unfortunately, the famed chamber filled with jewel-like salt crystals is not available to the public. But isn't the view of the underground lake, filling one of the excavated chambers, equally breathtaking?

Finally, let us have a look at the salt itself and go back to the old description of its three major kinds: *"Green salt. It is a large-grained type of salt … . It is usually mixed with traces of grey clay, and minute needle-shaped crystals of white gypsum. Although grey in daylight, it appears green when backlit inside the mine. Hence its name.*

Spiss salt. This is an age-old name, derived from workers from the land of Spiss, who are thought to be the first to mine it. This kind consists of thin rectangular crystals, dark grey in colour, and lamellar fracture. It glitters just like diamond. …

Shaft salt. This kind is found in layers below the two above mentioned types. It is commonly excavated through shafts descending from the interior of the mine, never directly reaching the surface. Hence its name. This

Wieliczka – a Jewel in the Polish Crown

is the purest salt, fine grained, with few impurities. ... Frequently forming large translucent crystals". (J. Mączyński, *Pamiątka...*, p. 286-287).

The Wieliczka Salt-Mine makes a lasting impression on its visitors. Children appreciate the salt figures illustrating the mine legends and history. Adults are impressed with wooden structures, large whims and other mining machines. All succumb to the beauty of great chambers and richly ornamented chapels.

The mine experience was even more dramatic prior to the introduction of electric light. Let us quote Józef Mączyński, who in 1845 published his account of the visit in the salt-mine: *"We are entering the Michałowice chamber, the vastest space of Wieliczka, what am I saying – the vastest gaping expanse nature worked out in the womb of the earth anywhere in Poland, Hungary, Germany, Alps, France ... . But here we come onto the balcony of this chamber, suspended close to the ceiling. From there, in the soft glow of an oil lamp you cannot discern the walls of this huge dungeon. But probe the darkness with your voice – you shan't hear the echo for a few minutes. This testifies to its immense vastness. ...*

In this abyss, dug with a brave miner's hand, ... our attention is attracted by a grand chandelier, made of translucent salt crystals, polished to glass sheen ... . During visits of distinguished guests, it is illuminated with 300 candles. This illumination – increasing the beauty and magnificence of Wieliczka's long corridors and large abysses by hundred – makes such a charming impression in this chamber, largest of all and carved out in the prevalent layer of salt, that it is hard to imagine anything more beautiful. And when the music is heard from specially-built gallery, or when the thunderclap of an explosion is carried by echo, we are charmed and succumb to awe, which no pen can describe.

All you can do is witness of these wonders, absorb them and reflect them in your baffled spirit" (J. Mączyński, *Pamiątka...*, pp 298-300).

Perfect all aspects. Nothing to add. Nothing to take away.

The Pieskowa Skała Chamber dating back to the mid-17th century, 27 meters in height.
The sculpture of a dwarf chiselled by Józef Markowski at the beginning of the 20th century.

◁
Pages 44-45:
The Janowice Chamber from the first half
of the 17th century. Life size figures chiselled
from blocks of salt by Mieczysław Kluzek in
1967, illustrate the legend
of discovering salt. A kneeling miner presents
a princess with a lump of salt
with a ring hidden inside it.

The Chamber of the Treasure Keeper, the main character of miners' legends. Sculptures by A. Batko, M. Kluzek and P. Cholewa from 1968.

The Dwarves' Chamber. The sculptural composition by Stefan Kozik representing dwarves working in the mine.

The Chamber of Casimir the Great, from the mid-18th century, with a 17th-century
Polish horse gear – one of the most original transportation mechanisms in those days.

Chamber named after the Wieliczka's chamberlain, Jan of Drozdowice – green salt monument to the Mine Carpenters (Antoni Wyrodek, 1967).

The Drozdowice Chamber from the years 1690-1743, one of the largest in the Wieliczka salt-mine. It is composed of two open-work constructions supported by pillars and linked by passages and galleries.

The Burned Chamber from around 1780, figures from 1972, made by
Mieczysław Kluzek, are a tribute to the dangerous work of "penitents" – gas burners.

◁
The Pieskowa Skała Chamber
– the old techniques of mine drainage.

The Erazm Barącz Chamber from 1864 is a salt lake featuring a foot-bridge,
and constitutes an interesting example of the old manner of securing excavations.

The statue of the Marshall in the Józef Piłsudski Chamber.

Kunegunda Transverse – the *paternoster* – a device for pumping mine water up to the surface.

Brine lake
in the Weimar Chamber.

◁
The Weimar Chamber – sculpture
of the Treasure Keeper chiselled out
by the miner-sculptor Stanisław Anioł.

St Kinga's Chapel. A Bethlehem crèche created by Józef Markowski
who, in 1895-1920, was the chapel's main sculptor.

The sculpture
of St Kinga
in the main altar.

A figure of the Virgin and Child
in the Chapel of St Kinga.

The Chapel of St Kinga – 101 meters down and one of the most beautiful of the Wieliczka Salt-Mine chapels. The chamber was carved out of green salt in the years 1870-1880. The chapel was constructed in 1896.

Niches with sculptures in the wall of St Kinga's Chapel.

The high altar featuring sculptures of St Kinga, as well as SS Joseph and Clemens – the work of Józef Markowski.

The Chapel of St Kinga. The Last Supper
(after the painting by Leonardo da Vinci)
– one of the salt reliefs (Antoni Wyrobek ,
1927-1932).

◁
The Chapel of St Kinga – figure
of the Holy Father, John Paul II by Stanisław
Anioł, designed by Prof Czesław Dźwigaj.
In the background – Our Lady of Lourdes
by Józef Markowski.

Unusually shaped salt dripstones
on the upper second level.

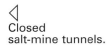
Closed
salt-mine tunnels.

Page 64:
Salt crystals from the cracks and caverns
of Wieliczka's famous Crystal Caves.

The Crystal Caves Complex was discovered
in the second half of the 19th century.

Salt crystals stand out due to their
startling cleanness and rare size.

Being placed on the UNESCO World Heritage list is usually a source of pride to the country and local communities which were granted such recognition. In this case, however, the situation is much different. Is it possible to rejoice, when faced with such a terrible place as the Auschwitz-Birkenau Concentration Camp, where mass murder of an unimaginable scale took place? The city of Oświęcim still lives in the shadow of that tragic past.

"The former Nazi death camp Auschwitz in Oświęcim-Brzezinka is the world's most recognized site of martyrdom and extermination. This camp became a symbol of the Holocaust, of genocide, terror, and the breaking of basic human rights. It is a stark reminder of what racism, anti-Semitism, xenophobia, chauvinism, and intolerance can lead to. The name of the camp became a sort of a cultural code word, describing the most negative human relations. It is also synonymous with the decay of modern civilisation and culture. ... For that reason the meaning of the word Auschwitz is both universal, as well as referring to memory and history of the many nations that became its victims." (Teresa and Henryk Świebodzcy, *Historic Outline* [in:] *Auschwitz. The Residence of Death*, Kraków-Oświęcim 2003, p. 6).

Soon after the Nazi invasion of Poland in September 1939, Germans started the planned repressions towards Poles, whom they considered "subhuman", and intended to use in the future only as a work force. First they targeted the nation's elites – the intelligentsia. Their intentions became apparent with the treacherous arrest of the Jagiellonian University professors on November 6, 1939 and their transportation to the concentration camp in Sachsenhausen. Soon, as a result of mass arrests, existing penal facilities became too crowded to accommodate the growing numbers of prisoners. The Nazi decided to set a concentration camp large enough to suit their purposes. The camp was to be modelled on the already existing camps in Germany. It was decided that the best location would be the city of Oświęcim, renamed Auschwitz. The site chosen was a compound of twenty army barracks, which could easily be sealed off the surrounding neighbourhoods. In the spring of 1940, Konzentrationslager Auschwitz was ready for the arrival of its first "guests". On June 14, of the same year, the first transport of 728 prisoners arrived. Initially only Poles were imprisoned there, but from the mid 1941 people of other nations were brought there as well.

The camp was, however, destined to play much greater role than it was initially designed for – it ended up upgraded from a detention centre to a full-scale extermination "machine", bent on the complete eradication of the Jewish nation. Poland turned out excellently suited as the stage for "the final solution of the Jewish issue". This was due to the fact that prior to 1939, it was home to three million Jews, about one quarter of the whole European Jewish population. The ultimate decision was made during the secret conference organized on January 20, 1942 in Berlin-Wannsee, where a plan of the full extermination of 11 million Jews was agreed upon. A precisely constructed death machine started to roll. It was to operate nearly until the last day of the war.

Directing several thousands of new prisoners to Auschwitz required the alteration of the camp. In the oldest part (Auschwitz I), new buildings were constructed and former single-storied barracks were elevated with additional floors. October 1941, saw the construction of a second camp in the village of Brzezinka (Birkenau). This was to be the largest of all the Nazi death camps. A new railway terminal – final destination for trains carrying Jews from the farthest corners of the occupied Europe – was installed. Housing gas chambers and crematoria, Brzezinka was also the focal point of the vast extermination machine. Technical support, together with the living quarters of SS officers and non-commissioned officers, was based around Auschwitz.

It is being estimated that at least 1,100,000 Jews, some 150,000 Poles, 23,000 Roms (Gypsies) and 25,000 representatives of other nations were directed to the Auschwitz Concentration Camp. Most of the Jewish prisoners (about 70- 75 percent), upon their arrival at the camp, were lined up for a selection and marched directly to the gas chambers. The victims were told they were being taken to shower. Locked in chambers, indeed made to resemble shower rooms, they died in agony, suffocated with the gas, Zyklon B. The killers did not only rob the belongings brought in by the Jewish inmates (50 kilograms were allowed per prisoner), but went as far as to remove gold teeth from the corpses of their victims. The German "industriousness" was also manifested in the usage of human hair – piles of them still traumatise visitors to the Auschwitz Museum. The bodies were incinerated in crematoria. During periods when the camp operated at peak capacity, they were also burnt in open-air pits. In the prisoners' accounts there are frequent mentions about the suffocating, unbearable, sweet smelling smoke rising from the crematoria chimneys.

During the initial selection, some of the people were chosen for forced labour – an inscription placed over the entryway: *Arbeit macht frei (Work Makes Free)* was not put there for nothing! There were about 400,000 of such prisoners, including 200,000 Jews, 140,000 Poles, 21,000 Roms, 12,000 Soviet prisoners of war and 25,000 others. All those prisoners were used as a free work force, ruthlessly exploited until death. Work was just another murder tool. Before dying, the victim was meant to bring profit to the Third Reich and to the numerous SS members on the camp staff. The camp prisoners died from exhaustion, from a guard's bullet or tortured to death in "medical experiments". But above all, they were deprived of all human dignity.

The prisoners adopted varied attitudes. Most of them gradually turned indifferent, subsiding to a feeling of hopelessness. Some co-operated with their butchers, torturing their fellow inmates (such cases were rather marginal). There were also attempts at resistance – counteracting the feeling of hopelessness and even active insubordination. Apart form the spontaneous actions, there were some organised attempts at defence. Underground conspiratorial groups operated within the camp. The heroic acts, such as the revolt of Jews from the Sonderkommando (the squad servicing crematoria) on October 7, 1944, are well remembered.

The extreme conditions sometimes evoked the most kindly acts, and led to heroism and saintliness. St Maksymilian Maria Kolbe – a Franciscan friar, who gave up his own life for that of another inmate, is a well-known figure. Today, numerous pilgrims visit the cell where he was starved to death. It is also important to mention Stanisława Leszczyńska, a midwife, who saved the lives of Jewish children born in Auschwitz. There were many such examples.

Only toward the end of 1944, when it became clear that Soviet troops will soon reach Auschwitz, did the Germans take action to obliterate the traces of genocide, to destroy documents, and blow up the gas chambers and crematoria. Most of the prisoners were evacuated into the Reich. The remaining ones were liberated on January 27, 1945.

Based on the Polish Parliament resolution of July 2, 1947, the State Museum of Auschwitz-Birkenau was established on the grounds of the former concentration camp in Oświęcim-Brzezinka. It is attended annually by some half million visitors from around the world. In 1967, a monument to the dead, with commemorative plaques inscribed in the languages of nations whose members died at the site, was erected in Brzezinka. Documentary work and scientific studies are continuously carried out here as well. The exhibitions presenting the extermination of all nations are updated. A very important and difficult problem is the conservation of buildings and exhibits. In order to illustrate these difficulties it is enough to quote some numbers: the Museum covers an area of 191 hectares and contains 154 buildings. Meticulous care of conservators is required for the wooden structures (e.g. the barracks in Brzezinka). There is also the problem of preserving the original barbed wire, surrounding the camp. And what to do with movable objects, such as the immense number of eyeglasses, suitcases and other personal belongings of the victims? We can only hope that they can be preserved and that the authenticity of this place is retained – in order to remember!

Museum at the Former Concentration Camp Auschwitz-Birkenau – Lest We Forget!

KL Auschwitz I. The camp's main gate features the cynical sign "Work Makes Free". Each day thousands of prisoners passed through this gate, sentenced to slave labour, which was one of the annihilation methods.

◁
Pages 68-69:
The Auschwitz II – Birkenau Death Camp. Railroad to the gas chambers and crematoria.

▷
An electric, barbed wire fence that isolated the camp and made it impossible for prisoners to escape.

Possessions seized by Nazi camp authorities from the victims, found after the camp was liberated. A fragment of the exposition in the "sauna" building.

A fragment of the exhibition showing, *inter alia,* the meticulousness of the procedure of admitting prisoners to the camp. They were registered, given numbers, photographed in three poses, shaved completely and dressed in striped uniforms.

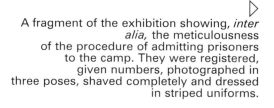

KL Auschwitz I, a fragment of the camp. In the foreground there is a double barbed wire fence, which was under high voltage at the time of camp operations.

Barracks of the former mass annihilation camp Auschwitz I.

Auschwitz I, Block no. 10. Here a German doctor, Prof. Carl Clauberg, carried out sinister experiments to develop a method for the fast, mass sterilization of women.

Page 74:
KL Auschwitz II. A fragment
of the camp's fence with watch towers,
which altogether was 14 km long
(Auschwitz I and Auschwitz II – Birkenau).

▷
Auschwitz I, a washroom in
which the prisoners had to strip
and were later led to the Death Wall.

TU WIĘŹNIOWIE PROWADZENI
NA ROZSTRZELANIE
MUSIELI ROZBIERAĆ SIĘ
DO NAGA
CZĘSTO KRĘPOWANO IM RĘCE
DRUTEM KOLCZASTYM

Auschwitz I, the interior of a crematorium, one of the places for commemorating and paying tribute to the camp's victims.

Auschwitz I,
a portable gallows
used by the SS to
execute prisoners.

Tins of the lethal Zyklon B, which was used to murder victims in the gas chambers.
It was supplied in the form of granules of diatomite saturated with hydrogen cyanide.

A fragment of the sculpture "Hunger" by Mieczysław Stobierski, comprising part of the permanent exhibit in Block no. 6, dedicated to the disgraceful conditions of the prisoners' camp existence.

A fragment of the permanent exhibit
in Block no. 4 showing a sea of human hair,
which was cut from the camp's victims.
After the camp's liberation in January 1945,
around 7,000 kg of hair was found
in the camp's storerooms.

The basement of the Block of Death, the starvation cell in which
St Maksymilian Maria Kolbe died, injected by Nazis with phenol.

Cell no. 21 in the
Block of Death.
An image of the
Crucified Christ
scratched on the wall.

Auschwitz I, a peep-hole in the door through
which SS officers observed the prisoners.

Auschwitz II – Birkenau,
one of the wooden barracks.

Auschwitz II – Birkenau,
a fragment of the camp.

Page 86:
Auschwitz II – Birkenau,
the interior of a camp latrine.

The interior of a wooden barrack.

Auschwitz II – Birkenau, interior of a so-called camp "sauna". Equipment for cleaning and disinfecting clothing with the use of steam or hot air.

A view of the former camp buildings. Nazis sent at least 1,100,000 Jews to Auschwitz, almost 150,000 Poles, around 23,000 Roms (Gypsies), 15,000 Soviet prisoners of war and 25,000 prisoners of other nationalities.

Auschwitz II – Birkenau, ruins of a gas chamber and crematorium no. III.

Auschwitz II – Birkenau, ruins of mass annihilation devices.

Auschwitz II – Birkenau, a wall of remembrance in the former building of the so-called camp bathhouse. It is covered with photographs brought by Jews deported to the camp from Będzin and Sosnowiec.

We cannot forget the victims of Hitler's Auschwitz-Birkenau Camp, the biggest centre of mass annihilation of Jews, the largest concentration camp for prisoners of other nationalities, a place of slave labour, mass executions, sinister experiments and pillage.

On the day of September 27, 1752 Their Royal Highnesses Augustus III the King of Poland, the Saxon Elector, with Her Royal Highness the Queen, together with the Eminent Princesses Xawier and Karol had their bison hunt here. The take was: 42 bison, in that 11 large – the largest of which weighted 14 Quintals [about 1400 to 1568 lbs] *and 50 lbs, 7 smaller ones, 18 cows, 6 calves; 13 elk – in that 6, the largest of which weighed Quintal 57 lbs, 5 female elk, 2 fawns, 2 does. Total of 57 beasts* (an inscription from a monument in the Białowieża Palace Park).

Among the Polish UNESCO World Heritage Monuments, one is particularly special. It reminds that esteem and protection is not reserved solely for human artefacts. This is the Białowieża National Park, classified as a World Biosphere Reserve.

Europe was once covered with vast primeval forests. The woodlands were systematically cleared to make room for farmland. Increased human presence and the accompanying demand for timber also took their toll. A sizeable decrease in their area was already noted by the Middle Ages. Great hunts organized for both food and sport decimated the fauna, bringing some species to the verge of extinction (see the opening paragraph). Centuries of such practices, with the added element of urbanization, depleted Europe's virgin expanses of grand primeval forests.

For a long time, the attitude people held towards forests was a rather utilitarian one. The woods were a store of natural resources to be exploited. The sooner the better. At the same time the grand, menacing forests demanded respect. There was the added element of the fear of the unknown – amply reflected in folk tales and legends. In times of Romanticism, the mighty, mysterious, and impenetrable forests provided a background and even became the topics of poetry and fiction. Artists also recorded the unsurpassed beauty of primeval forests in their paintings. With the recent development of environmental sciences, the large forest complexes started to be appreciated as a very important link necessary for sustaining environmental balance. This brought about efforts to establish protected areas where natural phenomena could take their natural course without any human interference.

One of such important territories is the Białowieża Primeval Forest – the last natural lowland forest in Europe. It is located in the Podlaskie Voivodeship, in Eastern Poland, by the Byelorussian border. A 10,502 hectare reserve has been staked out in the central forest. This includes 4,747 hectares of the so-called "strict reserve". The "Rezerwat" – protected forest district – was established here already in 1921. It was further developed into the National Park in 1932, and finally reopened in 1947 as the Białowieża National Park.

The Park stretches out on a flat upland moraine. Flowing through the Park are several small rivers: Hwoźna, Narewka, their tributaries Łutownia, Przedzielna and Braszcza and also the Orłówka River, which has its springs here. Forest takes up as much as 96 percent of the whole park area. It is a home to numerous trees; mainly spruce, scotch pine, black alder, common oak and birch. There are also: ash trees, lindens, maples, aspens, elms and hornbeams. Many of the trees grow to great heights – the best examples are the lindens, huge as oaks or spruces, reaching over 50 meters in height. Nearly 40 percent of the park wide tree-stand exceeds 80 years of age. Inside the Strict Reserve, since 1921 left to its own devices, the average tree age approaches 130 years. That is where the surviving stretch primeval lowland forest is located.

The Park flora is phenomenally diverse. In total, there are about 4,500 different species. Much of them are listed as rare and endangered. They include such specimen as: globe flower, Siberian iris, mountain arnica, holygrass and marsh violet. The most abundant group is formed by vascular plants (more than 1,700 species). Fungi, which constitute a separate group from plants and animals, is richly represented with three to four thousand species.

With over 12,000 known species, the Park fauna is even much more diverse. The actual species count is estimated at twice that number. The most abundant are insects (9,284 species), and birds – which form a substantial group of 250 species. Although mammals are the most modestly represented group, they include such majestic beasts as the European bison, elk, deer, doe and boar.

The reintroduction of European bison is considered as a great achievement of Polish environmental scientists. The last bison in Białowieża died in 1919. The species itself totally disappeared from its last natural habitat in the Caucasus in 1927. Only 54 animals survived in zoos. In 1929, the first animals were brought from Germany and Denmark to Białowieża launching the reintroduction process. Before the outbreak of the Second World War, the Białowieża herd counted 16 animals. The post war period saw a gradual increase in bison numbers, what allowed for creating free-roaming herds. The first animals were set free in 1952. As of 2001, 600 bison inhabit the Białowieża National Park.

Białowieża forest has always been a hunter's paradise. Great hunting grounds were frequented by Polish kings. Ladislaus IV built his hunting manor here, which was expanded during the reign of the Saxon dynasty. During the Partition period the Russian tsars used the palace as their residence.

The Palace Park deserves a separate mention – it encompasses an area of 47.77 hectares. It is an awesome example of an English styled landscape park and was designed by Walery Kronenberg towards the end of the nineteenth century. In the times of its highest prosperity, it boasted 160 types of trees and shrubs – both local and exotic, imported from Asia and North America. Today we can only admire 90 species. The Park houses numerous buildings. The oldest one is a wooden manor constructed in 1845. Unfortunately, the Tsar residence has not survived. It was burned down by retreating Germans in 1944. This impressive and picturesque structure, with two towers, dates from the years 1889-1893 and was designed by the architect Rochefort. The residence interiors were richly decorated. And during the period of the Second Polish Republic it was a favourite hunting lodge of President Ignacy Mościcki and his state dignitaries. It also attracted foreign diplomats and politicians, in the likes of the Hungarian Regent – Horty, Prince Charles of Romania, or infamous Hermann Göring.

Białowieża National Park attempts to cultivate the natural sciences and increase the environmental awareness of the Polish society. Walking and cycling trails have been established for tourists. There is also a trail through the Strict Reserve – tailor-made for nature lovers. It can only be visited in the company of a qualified guide. Naturally, the European Bison Show Enclosure is the foremost attraction. The Palace Park also contains the Professor J. Miklaszewski's Nature and Forest Museum. In 1999-2000, it was thoroughly modernized and brought up to the best educational standards. The year 1996 saw the opening of the Professor J.J. Karpiński Natural Education Center, which since 1999, together with the Museum, comprises the Białowieża National Park Education and Museum Center. The Center is visited by 70,000 guests annually.

We cannot forget about the Park's main scientific function. Intensive and carefully planned studies are being conducted here since 1920s. Among the numerous scientific institutions operating here are: the Institute of Mammal Studies of the Polish Academy of Sciences, the Białowieża Geobotanical Station of the Warsaw University and the Department of Natural Forests of the Institute of Forests Study. A very important role is also played by the Science Library operating within the Scientific Department of the Białowieża National Park.

A lot more could be written about this unique and beautiful place, where contact with primeval nature allows for a getaway from modernity, omnipresent technology, and the hustle of the modern world. Nothing can take the place of direct contact with nature, but for a start let us be introduced to the magic of the Białowieża forest through the stunning photographs of Adam Bujak.

Białowieża National Park – the Relic of Primeval Forest

The bison, Europe's largest mammal,
is a symbol of primeval forests. The animal
is featured on the coat of arms of the
Białowieża National Park.
Adult males, featuring powerful profiles
with humps, can weigh even up to 950 kg.
Females weigh up to 700 kg.

◁
Page 96:
Today's Białowieża Primeval Forest is a vast
complex with an area of 147,000 ha, located
on both sides of the Polish-Byelorussian
border. Around 60,000 ha of the forest are
found in Poland.

Page 97:
Primeval forest is shaped without human
interference. It is not subject to clear-cutting
and reforestation with cultivated seedlings.

▷
The bison is a species under
strict protection worldwide.
In 1996 it was added to the "Red List"
of species in danger of extinction.

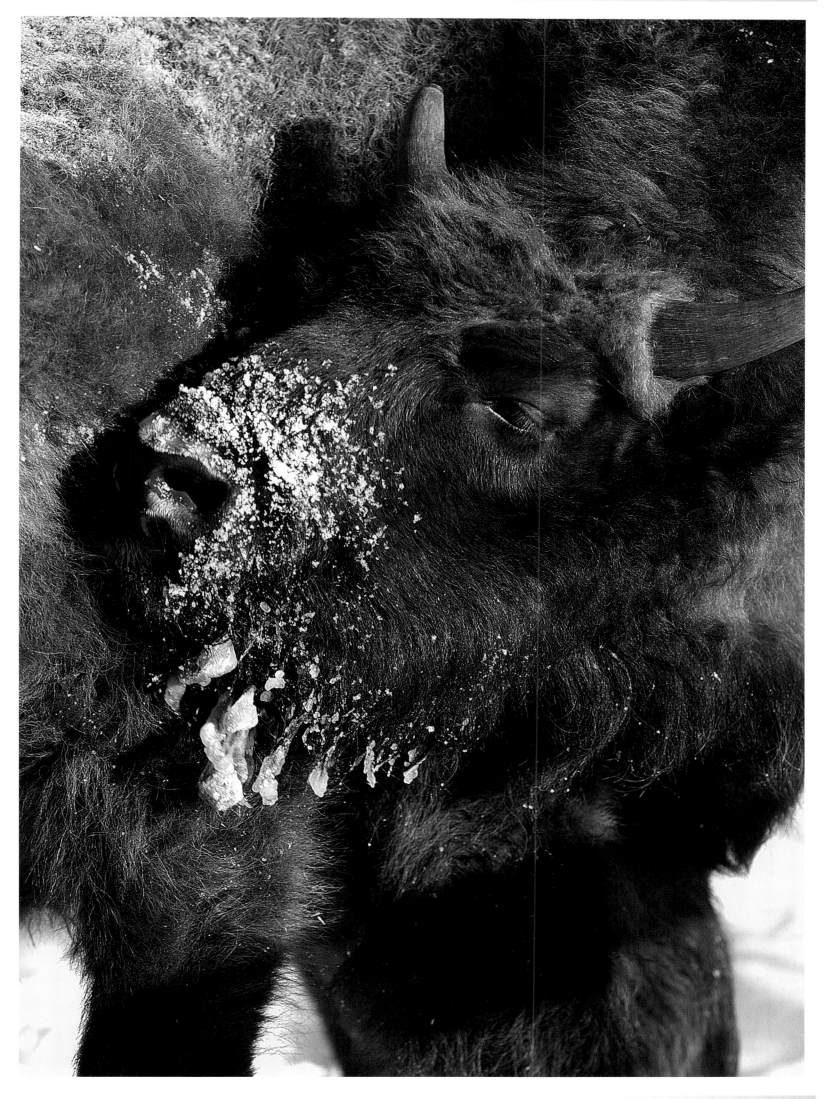

The extinction of Białowieża's bison began during the World War I period
owing to German soldiers and local poachers. The last of these bison fell in 1919.

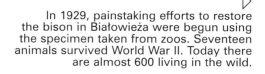

In 1929, painstaking efforts to restore
the bison in Białowieża were begun using
the specimen taken from zoos. Seventeen
animals survived World War II. Today there
are almost 600 living in the wild.

Three packs of wolves live in the Białowieża Park, comprising of 6-8 specimens.

The wolf is presently the largest predator living in the forest.

Does are not very common. In forest conditions they lead
lonely lives and only unite in small groups during winter.

Page 104:
The Church of St Teresa
of the Infant Christ – erected
during the interwar period.

St Nicholas' Orthodox Parish
Church from 1889-1893.

The oldest building in Białowieża – originating from 1845, the wooden former
residence of the Grodno governor. Today it houses the Natural Education Center.

People of different faiths
rest here side by side.

◁
A roadside cross
in a winter landscape.

DĄB

obwód 415 cm   wys. 34 m   wiek ok. 300 l.

WŁADYSŁAW IV

Wybudował zamek myśliwski w Białowieży nad Narewką. Wydana przez niego w 1641 r. Ordynacja Puszcz Królewskich wprowadziła ich ścisłą ochronę, a do Puszczy Białowieskiej wjazd był dopuszczalny tylko na podstawie pisemnego zezwolenia króla.

Monumental oak trees bearing the names of kings: Ladislaus IV Vasa and Augustus II of Saxony.

There are information boards explaining why these mighty trees, monuments of nature, have been given the names of rulers.

DĄB

obwód 415 cm   wys. 35 m   wiek ok. 350 l.

AUGUST II SAS

Wznawia w początkach XVIII w. tradycje świetnych łowów królewskich. Słynął z wielkiej siły. Kroniki piszą o nim: „Kłuł nożem dziki opłątane siecią, a żubry w dołach włócznią przebijał."

The wild boar is present in all parts of the
forest, particularly in damp, leafy woods.
It is estimated that there are between 800
to 2,000 boars.

◁
Page 109:
Well-preserved, large oak specimens
form part of the park's quaintness.

▷
Tarpan horses, bred in a half-savage system,
have preserved many primitive features of
their predecessors. Tarpans were completely
exterminated in the 19th century.

Deer particularly like forests
of varying age and species structure.

A deer's basic food in winter is tree bark and shoots.

An attraction of the snowy primeval forest are sledging cavalcades, completely forgotten in many regions of Poland.

A windmill, once a permanent element of the country landscape, today in the Białowieża Open-Air Museum.

A historical farmhouse featured at the Podlasie Open-Air Museum of Ruthenian Wooden Architecture.

Spring comes to the forest
later, and autumn faster.

An Orthodox roadside chapel
and cross in the open-air museum.

The architecture in the Białowieża
region is in perfect harmony with nature.

Deciduous growth called dry-ground forests prevail.
Spruce – the coniferous tree – abounds everywhere.

Deciduous trees grow close to rivers and streams,
frequently in the form of alder and ash marshes.

The bison lead a social lifestyle. Despite their mighty size, they can run at a speed of up to 50 km/hr.

In the Middle Ages, Warsaw was the main city of Mazovia – a region which long retained its individual character as an independent duchy, governed by the local Piast dynasty. Warsaw most probably received its city charter form the hands of Boleslaus II (d. 1313), at the beginning of the fourteenth century. Janusz the Elder (1374 -1429) chose it as his city of residence, and in 1413 granted it the Chełmno Laws. At the beginning of the fifteenth century, a settlement, called the New Warsaw was established on its northern outskirts. The regular, medieval urban arrangement of the Old City and the New – much altered, of course – is still apparent today. In the year 1526, Mazovia was incorporated into the Polish Crown. With its central location in the vast country, Warsaw often hosted Polish-Lithuanian monarchs, whose visits became more frequent and lengthy with the passage of time. After the death of King Sigismund I the Old (1548), his wife – Queen Bona, and in later years also Queen Anne Jagiellon took permanent residence there. After the 1569 Union of Lublin, whereby Poland and Lithuania were formally merged into a joint commonwealth, the Sejm (parliament) was moved to Warsaw. With the death of Sigismund Augustus in 1572, it was decided that the royal free elections would henceforth take place of the city's purlieus. At the turn of the seventeenth century, Warsaw became the residence of Polish kings, and at the same time it assumed the capital status of the Republic of Both Nations (the nominal status continued to be retained by Cracow). All those events greatly contributed to the city's fast development.

Keeping with the spirit of the Modern Era, various royal and noble residences were constructed in the suburbs of the Old and New Cities. They adhered to the *entre cour et jardin* model – with a representative courtyard in the front and a vast garden in the back. A splendid array of such palace-garden complexes was constructed alongside the Vistula riverbanks. The Royal Castle – residence of the king and the seat of the Parliament – was also expanded. Reign of the Vettin dynasty, left its mark in the form of the magnificent Saxon Axis palace and park complex (1713), and further alterations of the Royal Castle (1741-1746). The most significant changes took place during the rule of King Stanisław August Poniatowski. It would be hard to list all the ventures, carried out at the time, but let us just mention the king's grand projects in the form of the Royal Łazienki (Baths) and new furnishing of the Castle. In 1795, the capital shared the fate of the entire country divided between Russia, Prussia and Austria. In the nineteenth century, Warsaw was transformed into a modern city. With the 1918 liberation, it became one of the largest Central European metropolises. The city flourished during the Second Polish Republic. Public buildings of true artistic merit, were erected and scopes for further development clearly defined. All this ended abruptly.

In September 1939, the city was encircled by Nazi troops. Fury of their military prowess and state of the art weaponry rained down upon the Polish capital. Artillery and air force sowed death and destruction. Historic monuments, including the Royal Castle, the Grand Theatre, and the Primate's Palace were incinerated. The heroic defenders were forced to surrender to the overwhelming onslaught of Nazi forces. In the terrifying aftermath, 12 percent of the city laid in ruin. The toll of destruction was doubled during the brutal putting down of the Jewish Ghetto Uprising in 1943. Then in August of 1944, the Poles rose up against the Nazis. Deprived of any substantial support from the Allies, the Warsaw Uprising was doomed from the start. Adolph Hitler took cruel vengeance. From October 1944 to January 1945, special Nazi demolition squads roamed the city, obliterating anything left standing. Street by street and square after square, Warsaw was set ablaze by flame throwers. Entire city blocks were blown up with high explosives. An estimated 30 percent of what remained of the city was turned to ruin. The aftermath was horrifying. Some 700,000 of Warsaw's inhabitants lost their lives. 80 percent of the city itself was annihilated.

During the war, conspiratorial groups of Polish scientists as well as the museum and library employees of took up the challenge to save the Polish artistic and cultural heritage. They operated with the support of the Polish underground state organizations. Many treasures of art survived thanks to the heroic undertakings of people, who risked their own lives to hide them in (even if only seemingly) safe places. We owe a special mention to professor Stanisław Lorentz, who directed a group of people who saved a substantial part of furnishings from the Royal Castle, which was rigged with explosives. Thanks to his efforts, about four thousand articles survived the war, and were later used in reconstructing the site. Professor Lorentz organized the so-called "Pruszków action", utilizing points included in the uprising act of surrender, which granted Poles the right to evacuate cultural property from the capital. For two months, parts of the still surviving collections of the National Museum, libraries, archives and even some of the private collections were evacuated from Warsaw.

After the May 24, 1945 liberation, the Temporary Government issued a decree concerning the reconstruction of Warsaw "according to the will of the Polish Nation and to the standards of the reborn democratic State". The special Council for the

Warsaw – the Capital Annihilated and Revived

Capital's Reconstruction and the Capital's Reconstruction Office, were established to prepare detailed restoration plans. The Architectural and Historic Sites Department joined the Office operations. It was managed by Jan Zachwatowicz.

The first conception of raising the capital from ruins was presented as early as March 5, 1945. It was based on the pre-war development plans and studies worked out by the underground during the Nazi occupation.

The initial operations were random in character. The citizens of Warsaw spontaneously came out to clear debris from streets and squares. The period between 1945-1947 can surely be called a time of heroic reconstruction, great enthusiasm and hope for creating a new and better city. After restoring basic necessities, such as running water, sanitation and communication, the attention was turned, towards the end of the 1940s, to reconstructing the city's historic centre. The size of the task at hand makes it impossible to describe it here in full. A comprehensive synopsis of the end result was formulated by professor Jerzy Z. Łoziński:

"The post-war reconstruction..., carried out multiform, resulted in a new concise urban whole. Created in reference to its original state, it was nonetheless a brand new creation of a wide group of people, which included architects, conservators, painters and sculptors. The few structures to remain relatively intact – such as the buildings from the Dekert Side of the Market Square, and fragments of the old city walls – were returned to their original state by purely conservatorial means, with some new elements added. Most of the buildings, however, had to be built anew, based of their wrecked remains, old records, and photographs. Salvaged architectural details (or their copies), sometimes from entirely different buildings, were incorporated as well. ... A decision was made to return some of the reconstructed objects, such as the Barbican, the Cathedral, and the Castle, to their prime and original form. In the case of the Castle, it was re-erected in its early Baroque form, incorporating earlier fragments, and some of its subsequent additions. The interiors were redone in styles of various periods. ... The façade of the neo-Gothic Cathedral, was built anew according to a brand new design." (*Editor* [in:] *Katalog Zabytków Sztuki w Polsce, Seria Nowa*, vol. XI: *Miasto Warszawa*, part 1: *Stare Miasto*, Warszawa 1993, pp. XII-XIII).

The errors and shortcomings committed during the reconstruction are pointed out rather frequently nowadays. Political priorities of the communist government often resulted in decisions clashing not only with conservation ethics, but also with common sense. A good example of this ideological censorship was the replacing of old coats of arms, traditionally placed on buildings – and often having overt religious overtones – with new, "ideologically neutral" ones.

All these objectible imprecissions aside, Warsaw is alive and well! In spite of the criminal devices of barbarians.

The statue of King Sigismund III Vasa crowning the column in the Castle Square is the capital's oldest secular monument. (1644)

Tenements by the Castle Square. In the background, the towers and spires of St Martin and the Jesuits churches and the Cathedral of St John.

Old
Town's churches.

◁
Page 125:
The view from Castle Square to the tops
of the façades of the Jesuit Church
(1609-1626) and St John's Cathedral
(turn of the 15th century).

▷
The Church of St Martin
(1631-1636) and the old-town
buildings towards Podwale.

The statue of Warsaw's Mermaid in the middle of the Old Town Square where the town hall once stood. The sculpture was made in 1855 by Konstanty Hegel.

The spacious Castle Square before the royal residence.

View towards the Baroque façade of the Royal Castle from the Vistula.

The Old Town and part of the
defence walls viewed from Podwale.

Old-town fortifications with the Knight's Tower. Construction of the walls began in the first half of the 14th century and went on in stages until the mid-16th century.

The historical centre is surrounded by fragments of medieval fortifications. On the right, the Monument to the Little Insurgent.

The Barbican, the most interesting fragment of Old Warsaw's fortifications, rebuilt after the war. Note the four semicircular towers.

The Barbican was erected to protect the New Town Gate (by John Baptiste of Venice, 1548).

The walls of Old Warsaw – with towers and turrets – formed a double ring around the city. Here shown, the surviving medieval Knight's Tower.

The Monument to the Little Insurgent, commemorating the participation of children during the 1944 Warsaw Uprising – waged in defence of the Old Town.

The monument to Jan Kiliński, a famous shoemaking master and heroic participant of the 1794 battles with the Russians, during the Kościuszko Insurrection.

◁
Fragment of fortifications.

Tenement houses in Old Town
Square, rebuilt after the war.

View of Sigismund Tower of the Royal Castle from the perspective of Świętojańska Street.

The spire and tower
of the Jesuits' Church.

A passage joining the Royal Castle
with the Cathedral of St John.

Tenement houses in which a wealthy patriciate once lived, carefully reconstructed after World War II. Most of the houses are from the 17th century.

A favourite spot of Warsaw's residents and tourists visiting the capital.

A festive service held at St John's Cathedral with the participation of the Holy Father, John Paul II in June 1999.

The National Hall at the Royal Castle was designed by King Stanislaus Augustus. Celebrations associated with bringing the monarch's remains from St Petersburg.

The Castle's Conference Office featuring portraits of monarchs
contemporary to Stanislaus Augustus Poniatowski.

Page 141:
The neo-Classical sculpture "Chronos"
in the National Hall chiselled by Jacopo
Monaldi in 1782-1786.

A fragment of the Great Hall known as the Great Assembly Room.

The "Fame" statue in the National Hall by André Le Brun from 1783-1786.

Page 145:
The Throne Room featuring a royal throne standing under a canopy.

A hall, the walls of which are decorated with scenes of Warsaw painted by Bernardo Bellotto, known as Canaletto.

The Marble Room featuring portraits of Polish kings forming a frieze under the ceiling.

amość is a remarkable town. This may sound like a truism, but please keep in mind that had it not been for its specific qualities, Zamość would not have been placed on the UNESCO World Cultural and Heritage List in 1992. It is exhaustively described in popular tourist guides. Expert scientific studies analyse all the aspect of its history in great detail. So why is it so famous? Why does it evoke so much interest? What makes it so enchanting to both Polish and foreign visitors? To cut the long story short, Zamość is a remarkable example of an utopian model of a perfect town. But what does that really mean? The meaning seems to become apparent from the first glance. The urban arrangement and structures of Zamość were so carefully thought out as to perfectly serve their inhabitants.

Even though utilitarian purposes remained within the wide scope of attention during the city's design phase, it was not this type of "ideal" that was the primary focus of its creators. Ideal – means fully harmonious in a higher and symbolic sense of the word. In architecture, perfection is expressed by pure, unadulterated geometric forms. They have been attributed all sorts of various meanings since ancient times. Arranged together they formed a sort of a handbook, used by urban planners and architects enchanted by the idea of creating works equal to the unmatched creations of God himself. The challenge to design perfect towns, churches, palaces, strongholds, and also hospitals, universities and other public buildings were taken up especially eagerly by the Italian Renaissance artists. Italy is full of such endeavours. Some are more successful than others. Many have never been finished. Bernardo Morando (ca. 1540-1600 or 1601), author of the general urban design and of a significant part of Zamość development also

came from Italy. More specifically from Padua. He arrived in Poland – just like many of his countrymen – to find profitable commissions. After his 1569 arrival, he found employment in Warsaw, at the construction of the new royal residence. However, the greatest achievement of his life was made possible thanks to Jan Zamoyski (1542-1605), who in 1578 entrusted him with a commission, the sort of which is seldom proposed even to the greatest architects – the creation of a grand (for its day) city-stronghold, a centre of the vast latifundium and a clear demonstration of its founder and patron's grandiosity.

Jan Zamoyski is a figure shrouded in the aura of fame. He was an eminent senator, politician, commander, humanist, and a patron of science, literature and art. As the Crown chancellor, in many respects he set the directions for Polish politics during the reign of King Stephen Bathory. He made his mark especially during the interregnum, and the subsequent unexpected flight of Henri Valois from Poland. Commanding the loyal army of the lawfully elected King Sigismund III, he crushed the army of the Archduke Maximillian Hapsburg – pretender to the Polish throne – in the Battle of Byczyna (1587).

Zamoyski was highly educated. He studied in Paris, Strasburg and Padua, and composed literary works (including the Latin epigrams placed on Zamość edifices). He was a patron of the sciences and personally saw to their popularisation by establishing the famous Zamoyski Academy in 1594. This was made possible due to his enormous wealth – his estates covered 6,500 km^2 and brought him nearly 200 thousand zloty of income annually – a rather impressive amount by contemporary standards.

Let us get back from this tangent and concentrate on Zamość. Its foundation charter was issued on April 10, 1580. Construction of a city, planned for five thousand inhabitants, had to

be spread out over some period of time. The work of Jan Zamoyski, thus had to be continued by the successive lords of Zamość (such as Tomasz, direct heir of the great benefactor) and eminent architects – such as Jan Jaroszewicz and Jan Michał Link. Both of them were active in the seventeenth century and placed their mark on the city's current shape. The city, of course, did not survive unchanged to our times. It was significantly transformed in the first half of the nineteenth century, when many of the buildings were given a cold and austere Classicistic shape (one of them being the Town Hall). Also then, the Zamość fortifications were altered to make it a mighty fortress. Attempts to return the town to its past splendour were taken up several times. The original Town Hall façade was restored in the years 1936-1938. Attics of the stone tenement houses were restored towards the end of the 1970s. More work was done recently, prior to the 1999 visit by the Pope, John Paul II.

The city plan is formed on a pentagonal layout (slightly deformed due to the local topography), adjoined to a smaller rectangle. The benefactor's residence was located in a separate area. This exquisite building complex is today known only from paintings and illustrations. Using the Renaissance anthropomorphic parallel, it was the head of the urban organism formed to resemble a human body. The heart of the town is formed by the still surviving Collegiate Church (now upgraded to a cathedral), in which the great benefactor found his final resting place. A thorough observer, conscious of the Renaissance architecture ideals, will find the cathedral to be a realisation of pure, geometric harmony, where a visitor will find pleasure in taking in the numerous details and age-spanning furnishings. The artistic standard of the cathedral's past furnishings is seen in the former main altar – currently located in Tarnogród

Zamość – the Polish Perfect Town

– which includes paintings by the Venetian, Domenico Tintoretti. The town also boasts a vast array of other Catholic churches. There is also an Uniate Orthodox church attended by the Ruthenian minority, an Armenian church, and a synagogue for the Jewish community. The Town Square, also called the Grand Square (some 100 meters on side), which usually served mercantile purposes, was spoken of as being the town's navel. It was accompanied by two smaller market squares. The Town Hall, together with its soaring tower, symbolised the town's independence and administrative power, as executed by the City Council. Around the Town Square and alongside the adjoining streets, there are lavishly decorated "town square houses", ringed with low arcades. Next to the façades ornamented with proper, stencilled, Dutch styled, Mannerist ferruled décor, there are some buildings thickly covered with dough-like ivy leaves, and precarious figures of saints, looking as if sculpted in marzipan by some pastry chef, instead of an architect or a sculptor. Despite, or perhaps thanks to their naivety they cheer our eyes, sometimes provoking laughter with their comic shapes. They add a homely, provincial touch to this ideal, "Italian" city.

The city design was finished off with a partly preserved circuit of modern bastion fortifications, built on the new Italian system (symbolically perceived as the city's arms), with impressive gates modelled on the Roman triumphal arches. They were additionally strengthened by moats and an artificial lake.

Let us close this short presentation of the town with an opinion stated in 1598 by the Dutch humanist, Georgius Dousa: *"Nothing can better testify to his [Jan Zamoyski's] great love for his homeland than this city, which he constructed using his own resources. He raised it from the foundations up, fortified it with mighty walls and towers against the raids of enemies, and finally called it Zamość in his own name. He thus left behind a reminder, more solid then the pyramids and monuments, not only for Poland, but for entire Europe."*

Ground floors of town square houses are
ringed with low arcades.

◁
Pages 148-149:
The Grand Square – is among the most
splendid of the 16th century European
squares. The grid-work of streets
surrounding the market was designed by the
Italian architect, Bernard Morando.

The attic topped "Armenian" houses. From the left: The Wilczek House, The Rudomiczowski House, "Under the Angel" House, "Under the Couple" House and "Under the Madonna" House.

Institutions, shops and restaurants are currently located in these houses.

Chancellor Jan Zamoyski, the city's founder,
issued its foundation charter on April 10, 1580.
In 1618, Zamość was already being listed
among the most beautiful of
European cities.

The awesome Town Hall,
with a 52-meter tower and a grand
staircase, dominates over the Square.

The lavishly decorated houses: "Under the Angel" and "Under the Couple".

Façade of "Under the Angel" House with a relief showing Archangel Gabriel. Above, a dragon among ivy and a lion propped on his paws.

Page 156:
The sweeping, double stairway
of the Zamość Town Hall.

Page 157:
The Wilczek House is clearly seen to the
right of the staircase. It once belonged
to the councillor Jan Wilczek. Its corner
is embellished with a scene of Christ's
Baptism.

In 1591 – 11 years after launching the
city's construction boom – Zamość already
boasted 217 houses and 26 parcels.

◁
In order to accelerate the development
of Zamość, Jan Zamoyski issued special
privileges to Armenians, (1585),
Jews (1588) and Greeks (1589).

Monument to the Holy Father, John Paul II,
who visited Zamość on June 12, 1999.

Grand Square as seen from the Town Hall.

Former collegiate church, currently
the Cathedral under the invocation of Our
Lord's Resurrection and of St Thomas
the Apostle. View of the main nave vaulting
and impressive 25-pipes organ, funded
by Maurycy Zamoyski (1895).

Page 161:
One of the picturesque
nooks of old Zamość.

The Cathedral (1587-1598) was
constructed as a three-nave basilica
church. The interior was finished in 1630.

The tomb of Tomasz Stanisław
Zamoyski (1891), white Carrara marble.

The Cathedral was constructed as a token of thanks for Chancellor Jan Zamoyski's numerous victories.

The altar of the University Chapel with the image of St Jan Kanty, patron saint of the famous Zamoyski Academy professors.

The rampart was put up in order to prevent frontal attack on the bastion.

Fragments of the Zamość fortifications. The entire city used to be surrounded by moats, lakes and impressive brick ramparts.

The former
arsenal.

The New Lublin Gate from the years
of 1821-1822, and the post-Reformati
Church of St Catherine.

▷
The Old Lublin Gate was walled up
in the 2nd half of the sixteenth century,
several years after its construction.

just as in the past, so today it stands as if overshadowed by Gdańsk (Danzing) – the great Baltic Sea mercantile emporium. Strange, for it lacks none of its history, magnificent architecture, nor age-spanning works of art. It is Toruń, one of the most beautiful and important cities of the former Royal Prussia. Today, Toruń is mostly known for being the birthplace of the famous Polish astronomer, Nicolaus Copernicus, and for its gingerbread (*pierniki*), baked at the Nicolaus Copernicus Confectionery Plant.

The city owes its founding to the Teutonic Order of the Hospital of St Mary, commonly called the Teutonic Order. Knight-monks with black crosses on their cloaks are most frequently associated by Poles with brutal christianisation, raids, and pillaging of the Polish Crown lands. This aside, it is also fair to say that the Teutonic Knights exhibited great skill in founding and constructing towns and castles, and have to their credit the development of a well organised state. Their civilisational achievements are impressive even by today's standards. For proof, it is enough to look at the Malbork Castle or at the medieval structures of former Prussian towns, including Gdańsk.

In 1228, the Teutonic Knights received the Chełmno Land from Duke Konrad of Mazovia. They established, in 1231, a settlement in Toruń, which two years later obtained a city charter from the hands of the Grand Master, Herman von Salza. In 1236, the town was relocated in order to avoid the nagging floods of its original site. Owing to trade privileges, and a favourable location along the Vistula River, Toruń quickly developed and grew in wealth. In 1251, Toruń received a new foundation charter, which allowed for the town's expansion beyond the old city limits. In 1264, the New Town – with its own local government – was established nearby. Its 1280 entry to the Hanseatic League – a powerful trade organisation of Northern European mercantile cites was a clear sign of achieved importance. On February 1, 1411, a peace treaty – known as the First Treaty of Toruń – marking the end of the great Polish-Teutonic War and a victory of Ladislaus Jagiełło at the Battle of Grunwald (1410), was signed there.

The flourishing Prussian cities suffered under the heavy burden of the Teutonic rule. In 1440, in order to protect their interests, they formed the Prussian Union. Toruń became the seat of the Secret Council, who turned to Poland for help against the Teutonic Knights. And thus the year 1454 saw the beginnings of new developments in the history of the town. On February 4, the Prussian States rose up to throw off the yoke of the Teutonic Order. On February 8, the inhabitants of Toruń attacked the castle, took it by force and finally destroyed it. In March 1454, Old and New Toruń were unified into a single city, which in May of the same year welcomed the visit of King Casimir Jagiellon. In 1457 the King visited the city again, this time granting it new privileges and fifteen former Teutonic villages. On October 19, 1466, the Second Treaty of Toruń was signed, ending the hostilities of the Thirteen Years' War with the Teutonic Order. Toruń, together with the Chełmno Land, was returned to Poland.

The city's economic prosperity was based on well-developed commerce. Although located over 200 kilometres from the Baltic, Toruń's proximity to the Vistula allowed it to function as an inland port. Goods from Poland, Hungary and Ruthenia were shipped north, and those from Flanders, England and other countries moved south into Poland. The city's arable land and forests also turned out to be highly profitable. Craftsmanship flourished as well. Towards the end of the Middle Ages the town boasted some 10,000 inhabitants. The 1497-1500 construction of a bridge to span the Vistula (the largest one in Poland), designed by Hans Brandt, was seen as a sign of high civilization.

In 1520, the reformed faith arrived in Toruń. New worshippers systematically grew in numbers, in time ending up in the majority. Much later, Toruń witnessed numerous – unfortunately fruitless – theological dialogues between Catholics and Lutherans, the most notable in 1645. Sadly, there were also frictions and acts of intolerance. The so-called "Toruń Tumult" in 1724 ended with the execution of the town's mayor and nine inhabitants. It became widely commented in Protestant countries. The sixteenth-century Toruń became to lose much of its importance to the rival Gdańsk.

It would be impossible to relay Toruń's history in the little space available. We will end with this brief outline of its medieval glory. In its later history Toruń shared all the twists of fate which befell the Republic of Both Nations, culminating in the Partitions, when it was annexed to Prussia. In the twentieth century it became one of the most important cities of independent Poland. Today, it is a major science, culture and business centre.

Toruń is famed for its medieval works of art. Even though the later centuries delivered a rich assembly of architectural styles, Gothic still plays the most dominating part in this "symphony of styles".

The town itself overlooks the Vistula River. Although the port and piers of old harbour have since been replaced by bulwarks and riverside promenades, we can still admire a section of the old medieval defensive walls with an array of gates and towers. Among these are the Bridge Gate, the Sailor's Gate, the Monastery Gate, and the famous Crooked Tower – its "crookedness" stemming from

Toruń – an Inland Harbour

uneven settling into the clayey ground. Near the fortification, we come across the 1489 Townsmen Manor – summer lodge of the St George Brotherhood – next to which were once a shooting-range of the Bractwo Kurkowe marksmanship society and tournament grounds. The manor was constructed from brick appropriated from the dismantled Teutonic castle – of which only the latrine tower (*gdanisko),* with a fragment of the arcaded gallery supported by high pillars, survived.

Toruń still boasts the two market squares. This is a relic of the times before the unification of the Old and New Cities. The surviving Town Hall – erected in stages since the 1370s – is an impressive square structure with an inner courtyard and a high clock-tower. The recent renovation works helped to restore the beautiful original painted faux tracery to its red-brick façade. Only a part of the spacious building was occupied by town authorities in the old days. The rest served the purposes of business. Just as in Gdańsk and characteristic of most Hanseatic cities, Toruń used to have an Artus Manor – sort of an exclusive patrician clubhouse. Long gone, we only know it from historical sources.

The medieval Toruń had eight churches, of which only three are still standing. Perhaps, it would be better to say "as many as three!", because they are indeed the most splendid examples of Gothic brick work surviving in Europe. The Old Town parish church (today a cathedral), under the invocation of SS John the Baptist and John the Evangelist, dates from the second half of the thirteenth century. Its current shape is the result of numerous alterations done in fourteenth and fifteenth centuries. Its massive tower dominates the surrounding structures. It is the work of Hans Gotland, and dates from the years 1407-1433. The Cathedral houses many exquisite works of art, impossible to list in this short text. It would be unseemly, however, to bypass a truly magnificent stone modillion. It dates from around 1390 and is shaped to portray Moses surrounded by a wreath of flames.

The second Old Town church was raised by the Franciscans in the second half of the fourteenth century. The massive nave makes quite an impression in that it lacks the flying buttresses, so characteristic of Gothic architecture. How can such great and heavy walls do without support? The mystery is solved after entering the church – the buttresses were drawn inside.

The main church of the New Town, dedicated to St James, was built in the first half of the fourteenth century. The tall, elongated, and pinnacled buttresses around the presbytery, are extravagantly decorated. Another splendid characteristic feature of the St James Church is its spacious tower, covered by a double roof.

What other marvels await within the St James Church? What do the Gothic houses and granaries look like? Has Copernicus left anything behind? To find out, you will just have to come to Toruń.

Pages 172-173:
The medieval town along with the modern city – a bird's eye view. The city was established in 1233 by the Teutonic Knights. However, Toruń came under the rule of the Polish king following a local popular uprising against the Teutonic Order.

The Cathedral of the SS John the Baptist and John the Evangelist and the Church of the Holy Spirit as seen from the river. The Vistula River – the most important Polish waterway of the Middle Ages – was for a long time the source of Toruń wealth.

◁
The well preserved Gothic city walls and the 1432 Bridge Gate.

The Gothic tower of the St James Church (on the left) and the neo-Gothic
tower of the St Catharine Garrison Church (1894-97) – the city's tallest (86 m.).

▷
The Statue of Nicolaus Copernicus
(Friedrich Tieck, 1853), seen against
the impressive tower of one of the
largest and most exquisite European
Gothic town halls (1391-1399).

The Cathedral of the Saint Johns stands next
to the splendid Red Granary. It was originally
the palace of the eminent
19th-century town patricians, the Eskners.

◁
Page 178:
The Rafter's Fountain – according to a legend
he saved the city from a plague of frogs by
playing the violin. Edifice of the 19th-century
Artus Manor is seen in the background.

Page 179:
The New Town parish church under
the invocation of St James (1309-1455).
Its massive tower is uniquely topped
with two sloping roofs.

▷
Entrance to the Old Town's Town Hall. The
building is currently a museum space.

Page 182:
The Gothic Town Hall is decorated
with Mannerist turrets dating from
the years of 1602-1605.

The latrine tower, called Gdanisko Tower, is the only surviving part of the 13th-century Teutonic Castle.

The panorama of Toruń with the Town Hall and the churches of the Holiest Virgin, the Holy Spirit and Saint Johns.

Vestibules of
St James Church.

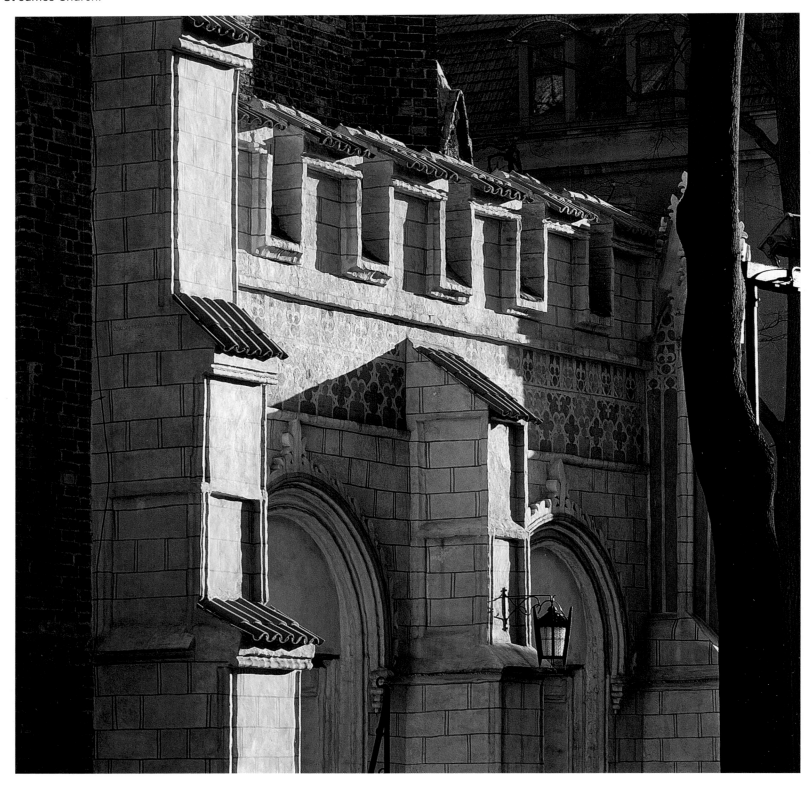

Recent renovation helped to restore colourful decorations to the vestibule of the St James Church.

View from the St James Church on a former, neo-Romanesque Evangelical church constructed in 1824. It currently houses a cultural centre.

Toruń boasts fragments of splendid and the well-preserved medieval fortifications.

Fragment of the restored defensive walls with guard posts. On the right, the tower of the St James Church.

A fragment of defensive walls and the Crooked Tower, dating from 1st half of the 14th c. The tower tilted soon after its construction. In the 15th century, Toruń was surrounded by a system of 32 towers.

One of the grand stained-glass windows (1898-1916) at the Church of the Holiest Virgin Mary.

The Cathedral of the Saint Johns – a Gothic bronze baptismal font (turn of the 14th century), with a Baroque cover. Nicolaus Copernicus was baptized here.

The *Tuba Dei* Bell (God's Trumpet) at 7238 kilograms is the second largest in Poland. Cast by Martin Schmidt (1530) in Toruń.

Page 190:
The gloriously radiant Annunciation scene – focal point of the Baroque high altar (1731-1733) in the Church of the Holiest Virgin Mary. Note the stellar vaulting.

The damned falling into the gaping jaws
of Leviathan – fragment of the Crucifixion
painting (before 1380). Cathedral of the
Saint Johns.

◁
Page 191:
The late-Gothic triptych with painted
wings on the Cathedral high altar (1506);
in the centre shown are the figures of
Saints: Wolfgang, Bartholomew and Jacob
the Elder. Seen above is a crucifix dating
from the 2nd half of the 14th century.

The Church of St James. Large Gothic Crucifix set in the Tree of Life (end of the 14th century), On the side altar, on the left – "Apocalyptic Madonna with the Saints" – wall painting dating from 1370-1390.

Fragment of the
Cathedral's southern aisle.

◁
Interior of the Cathedral of the Saint Johns,
the largest church in the city. Presbytery
covered with Gothic cross vaulting is the
oldest part of the church (2nd half of the
13th century).

▷
Page 196:
The Nicolaus Copernicus Museum
– the astrolabe reconstructed, according
to the astronomer's own description, by
Tadeusz Przypkowski and the Warsaw
Polytechnics staff (1964).

Royal Chamber of the Town Hall. Polish monarchs stayed here during their visits in Toruń. Picture-gallery of royal portraits painted between the 17th and 19th centuries.

A room in the Nicolaus Copernicus Museum.

ong gone is the glory of the Teutonic Order of the Hospital of St Mary, commonly called the Teutonic Order. Their Polish name *zakon krzyżacki* (Order of the Cross) derives from the black crosses after the Teutonic monastic brothers wore on their white coats. Although their mighty state is long gone from the map of Europe, the awesome red castle walls of their Malbork (Marienburg) capital – residence of the Grand Masters and one of the Europe's most formidable medieval fortresses – continue to tower over the Nogat River.

Even today, one can still see the brick Gothic town hall, the St John Church and gate towers, lurking among the city's housing developments. They are the relics of the medieval architecture, almost completely destroyed during the Soviet army assault on the Malbork stronghold between January 25 and March 17, 1945.

The mighty castle – a world-class tourist attraction – dates its earliest history back to the 1270s. The High Castle – a regular quadrangle with accentuated corner-turrets, and a diagonal passage running beyond the defensive walls to a latrine tower (called the Gdanisko Tower) – was already standing at the end of the thirteenth century. The keep was equipped with state of the art fortifications, such as the gate hidden in a triangular recess – allowing for defending against an open assault from both the flanks and from above.

The raise of Malbork came with the 1291 loss of Acre – headquarters of the Grand Master – to the Muslims. Defending the Holy Land – purpose for which the Order was established – was no longer possible. The knight-monks, however, had yet another crusade at hand on the shores of the Baltic Sea, where since 1226 they fought the pagan Prussians on the invitation of Duke Konrad of Mazovia. This turn of events allowed them to form their own state, constantly enlarged with lands annexed from the heathen. Power of the Teutons kept increasing, in time making them a principal threat to the neighbouring Polish Crown and Lithuania.

Malbork became the headquarters of the Grand Masters in 1309, with the arrival of Siegfried Feuchtwangen from Venice. The High Castle no longer sufficed, which launched a spree of rebuilding and alteration. In 1310-1312 the capitulary building – a huge two-nave hall covered with stellar vaulting – was erected. The Middle Castle also dated from that period. It included the Main Refectory dining hall. The new buildings also included dormitories for numerous guest knights, arriving from the West to aid the Brothers in their fight against the pagans. And not only pagans, after all, the Poles were already Christian for over 300 years.

A chivalric stronghold bearing the name of the Holiest Virgin Mary could not, of course, do without a place for the daily Eucharist. Therefore, the Castle Church was erected, in the years 1331-1344, within the walls of the High Castle. It was a rectangular structure with a polygonally divided eastern wall. The church was richly furnished with sculpture and paintings. It was unfortunately severely damaged during the World War Two. Currently, it is accessed through the so called Golden Gate, bearing the effigies of the Church and the Temple, as well as with the allegorical figures of the Wise and Foolish Maidens. A monumental figure of the Virgin Mary, located on the eastern wall, used to make a fabulous impression on the visitors looking at the Castle from the outside. Cast in artificial stone and covered with golden mosaic, it was unfortunately destroyed in 1945. Under the musical gallery of the Castle Church, there stands the Chapel of St Anne – the final resting place of the Grand Masters. Its two entrances are decorated with extensively sculpted portals. On the first one, we can admire the scenes of the Discovery of the True Cross, the Final Judgement, and Ascension. The second boasts images of various Marian themes (Adoration of the Magi, the Assumption, and the Crowning of the Virgin).

The most eminent part of the castle is the Grand Masters' palace edifice – one of the most luxurious and beautiful residences of late-medieval Europe. It was constructed in stages, assuming its final shape at the turn of the fifteenth century. Just as the whole castle it was built of brick, but stone was lavishly used in composing numerous details. Its towering mass was furrowed with deep niches, spanning almost its entire height. They were created by connecting the flying buttresses with arches, and contain vertical rows of rectangular windows. Pairs of granite columns, breaking up the buttresses at certain intervals, provide the massive divisions with an impression of lightness. The corners are topped with polygonal turrets overhanging atop oversized brackets. The walls are crowned with battlements and decorated with tracery blanks. The whole is covered with a tall sloping roof. Inside, the spacious, magnificently vaulted and well lit (through giant windows) summer and winter refectories, are among Europe's greatest works of Gothic architecture.

The extensive outer castle (called the Low Castle) boasted many utility buildings. There was a giant granary, supplying the castle's day to day needs, but also containing copious emergency stores to be used at the time of siege. The granary's ground floor was taken up by the stables, capable of accommodating up to four hundred horses. The Castle also had its own bakery, malt-house and brewery. Cannons and wagons were kept in the so-called *karwan*. There was also a smithy and a bell-foundry.

Malbork had a truly formidable system of defences. The High

and the Middle Castles were surrounded by a double, and in some places even the triple, circuit of walls, as well as by a moat. The fortifications around outer castle were chock-full with towers, the most impressive of which is the Water Gate. By medieval standards, these fortifications were practically impenetrable. In practice, the only way to take the fortress was to starve it into surrender, take it by deceit, or through negotiation. In 1410, the allied forces of Poland and Lithuania, who defeated the Knights at the Battle of Grunwald, laid siege to the Order's capital, without coming close to taking it. It was only in 1456, during the Thirteen Years' War, that the mercenary troops defending Malbork sold the Castle to the Polish King, Casimir Jagiellon. After the incorporation of Prussia into the Polish Crown in 1457, the castle became the seat of district starosts. It stayed that way until the First Partition of Poland in 1772, when the area came under the Prussian rule. In the practical spirit of the Enlightenment, the huge buildings were adapted for use as barracks and warehouses. There was even a short-lived plan of dismantling the castle. During the Romantic period, the medieval, intimidating, mysterious and partly ruined stronghold enchanted visitors. It found an important role in the budding ideology of nineteenth-century German nationalism, trying to adopt the history and accomplishments of the Teutonic Order as proof of age-old Germanic power and superiority. It was in this spirit that Konrad Steinbrecht started the meticulous restoration of the site in 1882. He organized architectural studies, restored sections fallen into disrepair, and took liberties in making the fortress all the more "historical", dressing the original Gothic structure in a neo-Gothic costume of his own design. The works continued for several decades. In 1923, following Steinbrecht's death, the works were taken over by Bernard Schmid, who continued the effort until the outbreak of the World War Two. The frenzy of Hitler's total war inflicted a terrible scar on the Malbork Castle. Soviet shelling nearly wiped it off the face of the Earth. Painstaking restoration still continues today.

The proud capital of the knight-monks – defenders of the Holy Land, who established a perfectly organised state on the peripheries of Northern Europe. The seat of Polish district starosts, who kept a sharp eye on Poland's claim to the land. A romantic reminder of the ancient and greatly "poetic" Middle Ages. Imagined proof of the great "Germanic spirit". A wounded witness to the storms of the twentieth century. All these are fitting titles for describing the Malbork Castle – a grand fortress shrouded in unexpressed mystery.

Malbork – the Capital of the Monastic State

The Middle and High Castles, seen from the east. In 1309 the Grand Master of the Teutonic Order chose Malbork as the capital of the newly forming, mighty Monastic State.

Boating on the Nogat River.

Pages 200-201:
Malbork – the fortress of Mary. The old
capital of the Teutonic Order. Europe's
largest Gothic fortress as seen from the
Nogat River.

View towards the Grand Masters' Palace
(on the left) and the courtyard of
the Middle Castle.

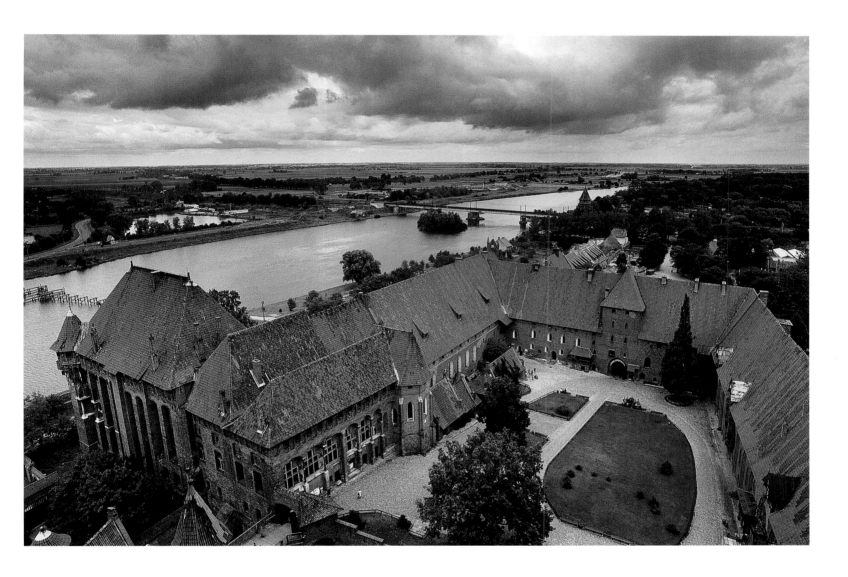

The High Castle seen from the south
– built as the monastic house, it is the
oldest part of the stronghold. The
Gdanisko Tower is seen on the left.

The Bridge Gate (1335-1344)
is shielded by twin towers. In the background,
a fragment of the High Castle.

The High Castle. Courtyard with picturesque
cloisters styled after monastic atrium. Open-
work lancets with brick and stone tracery.

Figures designed by Rudolf Siemering (Berlin, 1876), part of a monument commemorating the King of Prussia, Frederic the Great. They represent the four most important Grand Masters of the Teutonic Order: Hermann von Salz, Siegfried von Feuchtwangen, Winrich von Kniprode and Albrecht Hohenzollern.

Contemporary art exhibition
in the medieval cellars.

The High Castle
– the day room.

The summer refectory in the Grand Masters' Palace – the residence's most exquisite chamber.
The innovative radial dome (ribs radiating from a single point), supported by a central pillar.

The High Castle, the Chapel
of St Anne – a place of eternal rest
for the Order's Grand Masters.

◁
The High Castle – the capitulary,
a meeting place of the Order's authorities.

Kitchen in
the High Castle.

The Grand Masters' Palace, one of the largest and most splendid residences of medieval Europe.

The Knights' Dormitory – its low ceiling is supported by massive pillars.

Fragment of the fireplace in the High Castle's refectory featuring
a battle scene of the knights.

Fragment of the portal with
scenes featuring the Virgin Mary.

The 19th-century painting
in the capitulary presenting
the Virgin Mary and
the Baby Jesus.

The portal to St Anne Chapel from the mid-14th
century with the Coronation of the Virgin Mary.

The scene of the Ascension of Christ, on the
tympanum of the St Anne Chapel portal.

A bridge over the deep moat between
the Middle and High Castles.

The High Castle. The
battlement topped, four-
level residential tower is
seen in the background.

Basing on the 1466 Treaty of Toruń, Malbork was passed over to Poland and the Teutonic Order was forced to move its capital to Konigsberg. The Castle, henceforth, fulfilled the role of a starost and royal residence.

Courtyard of the High Castle. The late-19th century well house with a tall roof, crowned by a metal sculpture of a pelican feeding its young with its own blood (a symbol of the Eucharist).

The Middle Castle –
the spire of the infirmary.

A sculpture of the Virgin Mary
and the Baby Jesus
on the castle wall.

Page 222:
One of the entrance gates.

Page 223:
The Middle Castle, St Catherine Chapel.

riginally, the town was called Zebrzydów. Established and located around the year 1617, it took its name after its founder, the Cracow Voivode, Mikołaj Zebrzydowski, (1553-1620). Though, in about 1890, the town was renamed Kalwaria Zebrzydowska. But why Kalwaria? It is the Polish name for Calvary (Golgotha) – the hill, upon which Christ was crucified. The town would be nowhere found on today's maps, had it not been for its astonishing resemblance to the holiest sites of Jerusalem.

This is how it all came about. Mikołaj Zebrzydowski – frequent visitor at the Lanckorona starost's castle – decided to build on the nearby Żarek Hill the chapel of the Holy Cross. In 1597 his former courtier, Hieronim Strzała, returning safely from his pilgrimage to the Holy Land, brought his lord models of the churches erected at the site of the Crucifixion and over the tomb of the Saviour. The year 1600, announced as the great jubilee of the Redemption by the Pope Clemens VIII, seemed the perfect occasion to implement an act of piety. Thus came to stand the Chapel under the invocation of the Elevation of the Holy Cross, based on the Jerusalem original. The Papal Nuncio, Claudio Rangoni solemnly consecrated it on October 4, 1601. This is how the Żarek Hill became the Polish *Via Dolorosa*.

Mikołaj Zebrzydowski then took up an impressive task to render the whole vast area around the hill after the path the Saviour took on the way to His martyrdom. From the Cenacle, all the way to Golgotha. The idea, most likely came to him from reading the famous work by Christian Kruik van Adrichem (Dutch, also called Adrichomius – d. 1585), *Jeruzalem jakie było za czasów Chrystusa Pana (Jerusalem as it was during the Times of Jesus Christ)*.

The foundation charter, of what was to be Poland's first Stations of the Cross establishment, was issued on December 1, 1602 at the Wawel Castle. The document tells much of the founder's plans, as well as his intentions and motivations. It was written in Latin. In English it would sound as follows:

"In the name of the Father, amen.

For all times to be remembered, through this document let it be known to all, that we, Mikołaj Zebrzydowski ..., owing to the Lord's graces, have built ... the church ... under the invocation of the Holy Cross, modelled on the chapels from the Calvary Mount. [We have done this] *to evoke in ourselves, and in our heirs the memory of the bitter Passion of our Saviour, Jesus Christ, to whose deed of Redemption we entrust all our hopes for Salvation and absolution of our sins,* [desiring] *the eyes of our flesh to make our minds to unceasingly contemplate His mysteries and to give Him thanks and praise. Next to this church, God permitting, we intend to build, also following the Jerusalem model, ... the chapel of Our Lord's Sepulchre.*

... We have come to an understanding with the superiors of the Bernardines that, seeing how the holy sites of Jerusalem are in the care of the Friars Minor the Observant, it would be only fitting if the said Friars were to look after this whole area, together with the churches and chapels to be built here in the future, and the monastery as well."

The church and monastery were built in the years 1603-1609. Surrounded by fortified walls, against the attacks of bandits, they were designed by the Jesuit architect Giovanni Maria Bernardoni (with some changes introduced by Paul Baudarth). The monks wanted the new church to bear the invocation of Our Lady. The founder, however, insisted on consecrating it to St Michael the Archangel and St Francis. A compromise was reached and the church came to invoke Our Lady of the Angels, whose figure – brought by Zebrzydowski from Italy – stands on the high altar.

The work of staking out the Calvary (according to surveying done by Feliks Żebrowski) was started in 1604. The future locations of station chapels were marked by red wooden crosses. From the beginning they arose keen interest among both the locals and travellers passing along the nearby Hungarian tract. Many of them piously walked the path, contemplating Christ's Passion. The tradition of Kalwaria pilgrimages was born. It is still alive and well today.

Hills surrounding the Golgotha (the former Żarek) were renamed: the Olive Mount (Gethsemane), Mount Sion, and Mount Moriah. The Skawinka River became the River Cedron. The distances between stations differ from the Jerusalem ones. According to the above-mentioned Adrichomiusz, the whole *Via Dolorosa* was supposed to measure 944 meters (in reality 620 meters), while in Kalwaria it measures 1,288 meters. Chapels by the Kalwarian paths began to spring up starting in the year 1605. They were the work of the Antwerp goldsmith Paul Baudarth. Owning to architectural know-how, learned from his father, Baudarth was able to take up the task of designing the fourteen small structures, which are among the finest examples of Mannerist style in Poland. Some of them draw directly on existing Jerusalem structures (ex. Chapel of the Christ's Sepulchre), others are original creations. Many are very literal in design. The chapel commemorating the meeting of Jesus with His Mother, for example, has a heart-shaped layout. The House of Mary is composed of a triangle and trefoil, forming the silhouette of a rose.

The construction of chapels was continued by the son of Mikołaj Zebrzydowski, Jan, who held the office of the royal sword-bearer. The Chapel of Mary's Tomb, is among the structures erected at that time. Initially staked out in the early seventeenth century, the Paths of Passion intertwining with the Paths of Our Lady, were amended with chapels, built in the eighteenth and nineteenth centuries. There are over forty of them standing today.

Twice a year, they are the site of the famous mystery plays, during which scenes from both the Bible and apocryphal writings are performed. Vast crowds of faithful accompany Christ in his way to Golgotha on Good Friday. You can hear shouts of the Jews, cracks of whiplashes falling on the Saviour, and Pilate stating again his infamous words: *"Ecce Homo"*. Soldiers recruit Simon of Cyrene, to help the Condemned carry the cross, after He falls under His heavy burden. There are the weeping women and Veronica wipes blood off Christ's face. The Romans get busy preparing the execution. Nails are driven into hands and feet. Atop the Żarek-Golgotha the cross is erected. The massacred body of the Messiah is placed in the tomb. But the tomb is empty! All this really happens in Kalwaria.

An entirely different mood prevails in the middle of the summer on August 15, when the Church celebrates the feast of the Assumption of the Holy Virgin Mary. The hills and valleys are alive with song. The multitudes of pilgrims accompany the Mother of Christ to her symbolic tomb.

At the chapel funded by Michał Zebrzydowski and added to the monastery church in 1667, hangs the worshipped, miraculous image of Our Lady of Kalwaria. According to a legend, it cried tears of blood in 1641. His owner, Stanisław Paszkowski, gave it then to the Bernardine monks, who became its custodians. In 1887, the Bishop of Cracow, Albin Dunajewski, crowned it with the Papal crowns.

"Kalwaria Zebrzydowska: The Sanctuary of Our Lady – and the paths. I visited them many times, as a child and as an adolescent. I visited them as a priest. Most frequent of all, I visited the Kalwaria sanctuary as

the Archbishop and Cardinal of Cracow". These were the words spoken by Karol Wojtyła, paying – on June 7, 1979 – a visit, as Pope John Paul II, to this special place, situated not far from his native Wadowice.

Jerosolyma Zebrzydowiana – the Polish Jerusalem

Kalwaria Zebrzydowska is one of the most frequently visited pilgrimage destinations in Poland.

The Good Friday Passion Mystery – Jesus being indicted in front of Herod's Palace (the chapel dates from 1609).

Pages 226-227:
The Passion Mysteries
on the Paths of Kalwaria.

Chapels and the surrounding
pathways compose a uniquely
landscaped Passion sanctuary
– one of the most interesting
of its kind in Europe.

The sanctuary was funded by M.Zebrzydowski (1602). Apart from the church and the Bernardine monastery, he also commissioned chapels for contemplation of the Passion.

The Mannerist and Baroque churches and chapels spread over 6 kilometres.

The topographic and architectural
layout of the Kalwaria sanctuary
is a unique rendition of the
Jerusalem *Via Dolorosa*.

▷
Page 232:
Chapels and Paths were incorporated into the
picturesque Beskidy landscape.

The Western Gate – one of the oldest chapels, designed
by the Flemish architect Paul Baudarth.

Chapel on the Paths of Passion
– "Veronica wipes Christ's face".

The Basilica under the invocation
of Our Lady of the Angels and of
St Francis, as seen from the
"Golgotha" Hill.

◁
Chapel of Christ's Third Fall, funded
in 1754 by Franciszek Russocki.

Church of Christ's
Third Fall – interior.

Figure of the Virgin
at the altar on the
upper level of the
Church of Mary's Tomb.

The House of Mary Chapel (1612-1614).
The altar shows the scenes from Mary's life.

The image of Our Lady of Kalwaria is a copy of the miraculous image
of Our Lady of Myślenice, (painted sometime between 1633 and 1641).

"Ecce Homo".

Christ flogged while chained to a pillar
– a stone figure in the "Cellar" of the Caiphas' Palace.

The Kalwaria Church is surrounded by domed chapels. In the middle – the Chapel of the Miraculous Image.

◁
The miraculous image of Our Lady of Kalwaria "comes out" to the faithful on indulgence day – a feast celebrated on the Assumption Day (August 15).

The solemn Mass on St Sylvester Day (New Year's Eve) concluding the sanctuary 400th anniversary.
The rood-arch wall presenting a Kalwaria procession painted by Włodzimierz Tetmajer (ca. 1914).

View of the music choir supported
by pillars. The pipe organ funded
by Teresa Kamocka in 1706.

Silver figure of Our Lady of the Angels
– brought by Mikołaj Zebrzydowski
from Italy – is a centrepiece of Basilica's
late-Baroque high altar.

According to the Franciscan tradition,
the Bernardine fathers – keepers of the
Kalwaria sanctuary – put up an impressive
crèche (nativity scene) at Christmas time.

Page 247:
The main church nave and the façade were
funded by Magdalena Czartoryska and her
son Józef. The towers were erected in 1720.

The Kalwaria sanctuary is a centre of the unique
cult of the Virgin and of Christ's Passion.

The Church of Mary's Tomb (1615-1630)
funded by Jan Zebrzydowski, the son of Mikołaj.

hurches of Peace are an integral part of the Lower Silesian landscape. Their specific shape, construction, and name naturally come to make us wonder about their origin.

In the years 1618-1648, a violent and exhausting war, known as the Thirty Years' War raged across Europe. The countries allied together in the Catholic League clashed with the forces of those allied in the Protestant Union. The hostilities ceased with the signing of a peace treaty on October 24, 1648 in Münster and Osnabrück. It is known as the Peace of Westphalia. The treaty ratified the then-common rule of *cuius regio, eius religio*, according to which the ruler decided about his subjects religion.

It is common knowledge, that the majority of lands constituting the Hapsburg Empire were inhabited by Protestants. Such was the case in Silesia. Following the introduction of the Reformation into the region, Catholic churches were converted into Protestant ones. The Emperor decided, however, to return them to the Catholic worshippers. For his wide-spread re-catholisation action he engaged monastic orders, such as the Jesuits, who were settled in the Świdnica parish-church. The Gothic churches were garnished with exquisite Baroque furnishings. This was supposed to emphasize the superiority of Roman-Catholic faith over the reformed one. Paintings and sculpture constituted a part of a controversial program with anti-Protestant undertones.

It was only in the year 1652, that Ferdinand III agreed for the construction of three Lutheran churches in Silesia. These were to be located in Świdnica, Jawor and Głogów (the latter did not survive). The conditions set down by the Emperor for this concession were extremely harsh. The churches were to be located outside the town walls (at a cannon-shot's distance), they could not resemble the Catholic churches, nor could they possess steeples, and most importantly, they could not be built from any lasting materials such as brick and stone. Finally, the span of the construction work could not exceed one year.

In order to gather funds necessary for their construction, the Silesian communities turned for help to their brethren in Protestant countries. Albrecht von Saebisch (1610-1668), a Breslau architect, was engaged to prepare their designs. Construction in Jawor begun on April 24, 1654 and the consecration took place towards the end of the following year. The corner-stone in Świdnica was laid down on August 23, 1656, and the first ceremony was held there on June 24, 1657.

Following the Imperial restrictions, Churches of Peace were built on a timber-frame construction, with wattle-and-daub infill. The Jawor church is a three aisled basilica, topped in 1707 with a steeple (after the treaty in Altransztat). The Świdnica church was laid out on a Greek cross design. The investors' goal was to construct a building spacious enough to house the large congregations in time of prayer. This was achieved in a rather clever fashion by introducing tiered galleries into the church interiors. Owing to this solution – a characteristically Protestant one – the church in Świdnica can house as many as 7,500 worshippers, and the one in Jawor – 6,000.

Lutheran places of worship tend to be very modestly decorated. Their modesty often contrasted the splendour of Catholic churches. The Churches of Peace, however, are extensively decorated, with images painted on ceilings, walls and gallery railing. We can thus admire – in Jawor – scenes and quotations from the Old and New Testaments, illustrating the world history as seen through the prism of God's redemption plan (painted by Georg Flegel from Kowary). The Old Testament figures and stories act as antecedents to the characters and events found in the New Testament. The ceiling of the Świdnica church presents us with an image of the Holy Trinity and other scenes illustrating the visions described by St John the Evangelist in the Book of Revelation (executed by Christian Suessenbach and Christian Kolitschky). Additionally, the church interiors bear the coats of arms of eminent congregation members, who used to sit in private stalls separate from the galleries. Decorations are supplemented with views of neighbouring towns and residences.

The main elements of the Lutheran church furnishings are: an altar where the Mass is said, a pulpit from which the sermon is delivered, and a font for providing the sacrament initiating a new member into the Christian community.

An altar retable in the Jawor church was executed in 1672 by Martin Schneider from Kamienna Góra. Initially it housed an image of the Last Supper, which was replaced, in 1854, by the image of Christ in the Garden of Gethsemane. It is framed with sculptures of Moses and St John the Baptist. The pulpit, with figures portraying the four Evangelists is the work of Mathäus Knote from Legnica, and dates from 1670. The font dates from 1656.

The late-Baroque altar (1752) and pulpit (1729) in Świdnica, are the works of a local wood-carver, Gottfried August Hoffman. Especially noteworthy is the altar retable with sculptures showing the scene of Christ being baptised by St John the Baptist and others portraying the Old and New Testaments' characters: Moses with Aaron and SS Peter and Paul. A figure of the Lamb dominates the whole, and the Last Supper can be seen in the predella. A font, dating from 1661 – and executed by Pankratius Werner from Jelenia Góra – is located in a room added to the main nave from the east. This room also houses 40 portraits of the congregation pastors.

The chorus accompanied by organ music plays a very important role in the Lutheran Church liturgy. A magnificent organ is frequently the most eminent element of the church interiors. The Świdnica church boasts two such instruments. The larger, dating from the years of 1666-1669 is the work of organ-master Christoph Klose from Brzeg. The smaller dates from 1695, and is located over the altar. The organ in Jawor is much younger. It was constructed in 1855 by Andreas Lummert from Breslau, and later altered by Heinrich Schlag in 1896.

From a purely artistic standpoint, it would be hard to consider the Churches of Peace as masterpieces. They are none the less extraordinary. It should be noted that despite their seemingly weak construction, they have already survived over three and a half hundred years. Most important though, is their spiritual meaning. During their construction in the seventeenth century, the Protestant community was overjoyed, but numerous Catholics looked at the endeavour with sadness and often with anger. The humiliating constraints that were imposed as a condition of their construction were a slap in the face of the Lutheran community. Back then, the Emperor's grace was not seen as a sign of tolerance towards a different faith, but rather as a temporary weakness of the ruling authority in imposing its own faith on the subjects. Today, they stand as true symbols of peace stemming from the understanding between people of various faiths. In 1989, the Świdnica church, welcomed two eminent guests. The Polish Prime Minister, Tadeusz Mazowiecki, and the German Chancellor, Helmut Kohl, stopped there on their way to a meeting in Krzyżowa. Together they prayed for reconciliation of Polish and German nations and for the peaceful future of Europe.

"History cannot be reversed. We are, however, challenged by the lessons we are ready to learn from it for the benefit of the present and for the future of our children. This is a worthy mission for the Holy Trinity Church of Peace. And today, it should be remembered with gratitude, that after all rejections and disdain of the past, there is now the will to jointly proclaim the Lord's grace in the Evangelical-Lutheran and Roman-Catholic Churches. As a representative of the World Community of the Lutheran Churches – which includes the Evnagelical-Augsburg Church in Poland – I placed, in 1999 in Augsburg on the feast of Reformation – my signature confirming "the joint declaration of learning to excuse" with the Roman-Catholic Church. I also wish to emphasise here, in Świdnica, the hope to develop a common dialogue between our Churches. The Polish Pope, John Paul II called this declaration "a milestone on a challenging road to the renewed unity of Christians", (quote from a sermon delivered on September 8, 2002 by the Bishop Christian Krause, President of the World Lutheran Federation, during the ceremony of the 350th anniversary of the completion of the Świdnica church).

Churches of Peace in Jawor and Świdnica

Pages 250-251:
The Church in Jawor. Interior
of a timber-frame structure,
surrounded by four levels
of wooden galleries, and boxes
of nobility and craftsmen guilds.

The church can accommodate up to
6,000 worshippers; on the photograph,
pipe organs from ca. 1855.

◁
A view towards the 1672 high altar by Martin
Schneider and galleries decorated with paintings
representing biblical scenes, heraldic motifs and
the nobility's ancestral abodes.

▷
Page 254:
The exceptional architecture is the work
of Albrecht von Saebisch and the
masterly woodwork is by Andreas Gamper.

A labyrinth of passages in the galleries. The coffered ceiling
is covered by a blue wall painting with floral ornaments.

The galleries contain many
original Baroque and Rococo seats.

The figure of the Resurrected
Christ crowns the pulpit.

An angel
holding the
gospel supports
the pulpit.

◁
Page 256:
The oldest element of the interior is the
baptismal font dating back to 1656, funded
by Anna and George von Schweinitz.

Page 257:
The top part of the richly decorated pulpit by
Matthäus Knote (1670).

The church is filled with many epitaphs dedicated to the memory of wealthy Silesian nobility.

Flagellation
– one of the paintings decorating the pulpit.

The Arrest of Jesus
– part of the pulpit decoration.

King David – paining
on the confessional
(unusual furnishing
of a Protestant church).

Construction of the Church was subject to restrictions. It had to be situated outside the city walls, it could not resemble Catholic churches, and had to be constructed of wood and clay.

◁
The Lutheran Church of Peace under the invocation of the Holy Spirit in Jawor was erected in 1654-1655.

The Church of Peace in
Świdnica is patterned on the cross.

View from the music choir towards
the late-Baroque high altar and galleries.

The impressive pipe organ dating back to 1666-1669 –
the work of organ master Christoph Klose from Brzeg.

Crest of the high altar and the small organs above the altar (1695).

View towards the main aisle and altar. The church can accommodate up to 7,500 people.

The exquisitely decorated box
of the Hochberg family.

◁
The high altar from 1752 by local wood-
carver Gottfried August Hoffman.

▷
Page 270:
The Personification of Faith
– a fragment of the pulpit's decoration.

The Hochbergs' coat of arms seen in the family's box.

Prominent members of the Lutheran congregation were commemorated with splendid epitaph plaques.

"The Destruction of Jerusalem"
– fragment of the ceiling painting
portraying scenes from the Book
of Revelation.

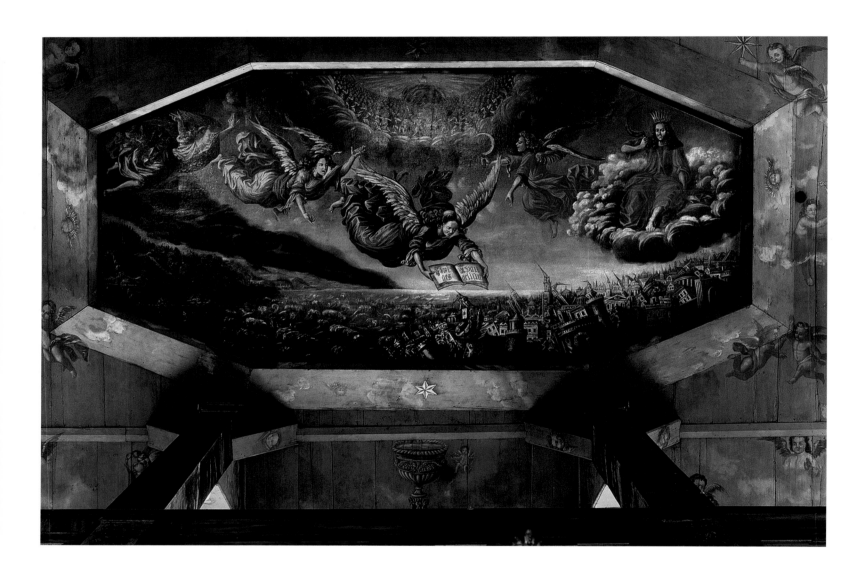

◁
Page 272:
The unique Churches of
Peace attract many visitors.

Page 273:
Narrow, winding stairs leading to the gallery.

▷
"Opening of the Last Seal" – fragment
of the ceiling painting by Christian
Suessenbach and Christian Kolitschky.

The Lutheran church
was erected in 1656-1657.

Churches of Peace are unusual relics
– despite a seemingly fragile structure, they
have already survived over 350 years.

The proud expression "monument of architecture" is commonly associated with monumental, stone and brick edifices – the works of famous architects. Impressive temples, palaces, public buildings, astonishing feats of engineering undoubtedly deserve admiration and recognition. There are, however, structures far off from the famed world art centres – in the provinces and seldom visited regions – which still evoke true admiration.

For hundreds of years Polish landscape was dominated by wooden architecture. Palaces, aristocratic manors, tenement houses, peasant cottages, mills, barns, churches, and synagogues. Numerous towns, not to mention villages, were – as recent as the early twentieth century – comprised entirely of wooden structures. So what happened with all those awesome timber works of art? How was it possible that in the twentieth century wood was nearly completely obliterated from our towns and villages? The havoc and devastation was brought on by the two World Wars. Progress is also to blame. Even today, wooden architecture is associated with primitive backwardness. Therefore, in the name of true, or supposed progress, all obsoleteness was uprooted. In order to really estimate the colossal changes, it is enough to look at the old photographs of Polish villages from the 1950s and 60s, and then compare them with their present state. The lost visions of idyll cottages framed in malva flowers peeking over the wooden fences are heart–wrenching, but we have to accept the rights of their inhabitants to live in modern brick houses. But how can it be that all those wooden churches, meticulously cared for by the local communities for hundred centuries, disappear before our eyes? Is prayer any better in the new brick structures raised next to the old? It is perhaps more comfortable, but hardly better. Every once in a while we hear of yet another wooden church burning down, often as result of vandalism or arson. It is not uncommon to come across a cosy little wooden church overshadowed by a new brick and concrete structure, abandoned by parishioners, padlocked and slowly decaying.

We are, however, fortunate enough to still find places where tradition is respected and a watchful eye is kept on the thin thread binding us to our ancestry There are people who will do much to preserve the scarce and vanishing traces of culture, for the generations to come. Owing to their efforts, this part of our national heritage was noticed by the international community, which decided that a selected group of wooden churches in Southern Poland deserves to be put on the World Cultural and Natural Heritage List.

There prevails a common notion that wooden architecture belongs to folk art. This is a rather deceiving idea, both in the case of the Gothic and as well as the modern wooden churches. Above all, these were the works of highly skilled guild carpenters.

The churches, honoured by UNESCO are located in the area of Podkarpackie Voivodeship – in Blizne, Haczów, Binarowa, and Małopolskie Voivodeship – in Dębno, Lipnica Murowana, Sękowa. The oldest one – in Haczów – is the church under the invocation of the Assumption of the Holiest Virgin Mary and St Michael the Archangel. It dates back to the last quarter of the fourteenth century. Other churches were constructed in the mid-fifteenth century (All Saints' Church in Blizne, and St Michael the Archangel in Dębno) or at the turn of the sixteenth century (St Leonard's in Lipnica Murowana, SS Philip and James in Sękowa, and St Michael the Archangel in Binarowa). A characteristic feature of all these temples is their log construction. Their walls are constructed of huge logs, joined and then covered with boarding or siding. Their spatial arrangement is fairly simple – nave on a square type layout, joined with a rectangular, polygonally closed presbytery. Some of the churches also have towers. A particularly southern Polish touch are the rafters over the side parts of nave. Their presence stems from the fact that both the presbytery and the nave are covered with a single roof. The shape of wooden churches is reminiscent of small Gothic churches, which doubtlessly served as their models.

Only few of the churches retained any of their original furnishing. Artistic value of paintings from Haczów (1494) is immeasurable. The rich stencilled décor in the Dębno church (ca. 1500) is also well preserved. It is dominated by geometric shapes and flower motifs, with the Eagle – an emblem of the Polish Crown – and a deer hunting scene, springing up unexpectedly in the midst of them. The Dębno church is exquisitely furnished. Here we can see a Crucifix in the rood-arch (1380), a late-Gothic triptych dating from the beginning of the sixteenth century and a Gothic pulpit – a true rarity. In the Cracow Archdiocese Museum, we can currently view a fragment of a late-thirteenth century image found in Dębno – the oldest relic of panel painting surviving in Poland. A couple of years ago, the church in Lipnica Murowana was still decorated with splendid late-Gothic altars. They were unfortunately stolen. Eventually recovered, they were transferred to the Diocese Museum in Tarnów for safekeeping.

The churches described here compose a beautiful sample of the numerous preserved wooden architecture sites of Poland. They are especially abundant in the Małopolskie Voivodeship. Towards the end of 1990s an interesting idea arose to make them accessible through the means of conveniently marked, described and promoted tourist routes. The result was the Trail of Wooden Architecture. Similar efforts were undertaken in the neighbouring Silesian and Podkarpackie Voivodeships. In total, the trail is to span over 1,500 kilometres and include 232 of the most precious sites. These include 123 Catholic churches, 39 Orthodox churches and 14 manor houses.

It is apt to express our hope that this, as well as similar initiatives, will help to bring the splendid works of wooden architecture to wider audiences, and build awareness to the burning need to save and preserve them for posterity.

Wooden Churches of Southern Poland

A panoramic view of Binarowa with
the Church of St Michael the Archangel.

◁
Pages 280-281:
Dębno Podhalańskie – wooden framework
churches of Małopolska recall the form
of brick Gothic churches.

▷
View from the gate towards
the church's tower.

The church rafters – a view towards the presbytery
and side altar as seen from the music choir.

The side chapel of Our Lady and the Guardian Angels
with an altar honouring the Virgin.

"Crowning with Thorns" – fragment of the 17th-century wall
painting portraying Christ's Passion on the northern wall of the presbytery.

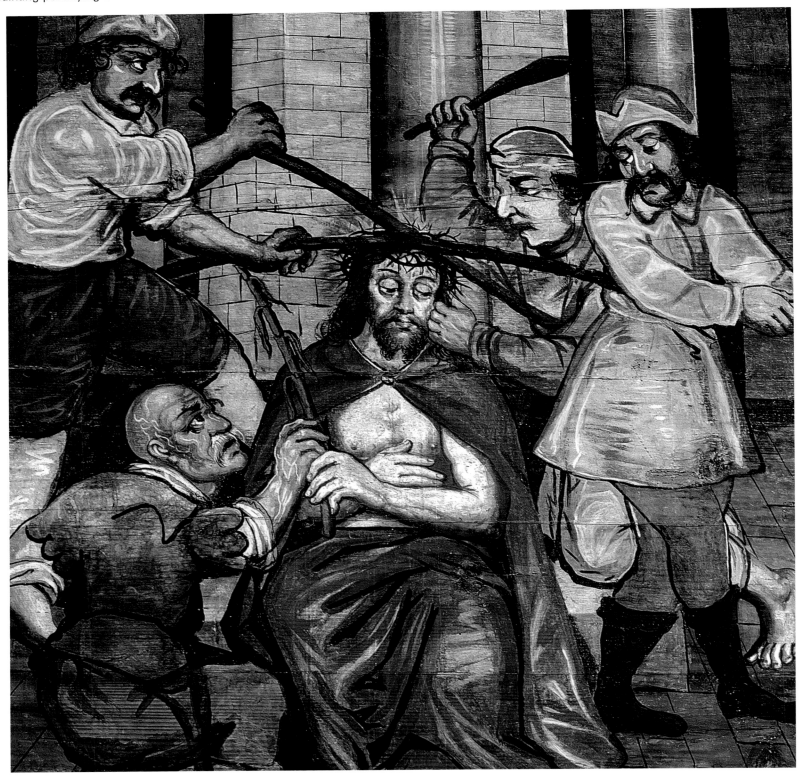

Page 284:
View towards the choir and the
exquisite 17th-century wall painting.

"Ecce Homo" – fragment of wall paining portraying the Passion scenes.

The high altar figure of the Virgin and Child (2nd quarter of the 15th cent.).

The Blizne village was established
by King Casimir the Great in 1366.

◁
The Church of All Saints in Blizne.
It is one of Poland's most precious
relicts of late-medieval, sacral
wooden architecture.

The church was most likely
built sometime between 1406-1470.

Sacristy walls and ceiling
are decorated with
paintings dating back
to the early 18th century.

Early 18th-century high altar with an image portraying the Saints in Adoration of the Virgin.

View of the presbytery and two side altars.
On the left, a late-Gothic figure of the
Madonna – Holy Mary Full of Grace.

◁
A wooden baptismal font (early 18th cent.),
supported by a figure of an angel.

Church under the invocation of the
Holiest Virgin Mary and of St Michael
the Archangel in Haczów. It was
constructed of fir (rare in these parts).

The main gate and belfry.
The Haczów Church is traditionally
linked with Queen Hedwig.

The miraculous figure of Our Lady
of Sorrows (early 15th century).

Head of the Crucified
Christ – from the
rood-beam (fragment).

Vernicle (Christ's face on a veil) – fragment of
a late-Gothic wall paining over the nave's entrance.

Interior of the Church in Dębno
Podhalańskie. This most famous
of Polish wooden churches is furnished
in splendid Gothic works of art.

▷
Walls and ceiling of the church
are covered with colourful geometric,
floral and heraldic motifs.

The Church in Lipnica Murowana. Crucifix from the rood-beam (ca. 1380) and original paintings dating from around 1500. The high altar features the triptych presenting Saints: Leonard, Laurence and Florian (ca.1500). On the left, the triptych "Adoration of the Infant Jesus" (ca. 1475).

The antique pulpit
with painted images
of the four Evangelists.
Staircase railing
is decorated in
subtle floral motifs.

Christ from the Crucifixion
group set in the rood-arch.

A view of the church
from the cemetery.

The floral medallions
showing the scenes
of Christ's Passion.

The presbytery walls are covered with figurative paintings dating from the 16th and 17th centuries. Northern wall is embellished with the portrayal of the Final Judgement.

The Gothic Church under the invocation
of SS Philip and James the Apostle
in Sękowa (made of larch, ca. 1520).

The church and the entrance gate seen from
the east. The nave, presbytery and sacristy
are covered by a single, very steep roof,
covered with shingles.

Death of the Virgin – scene
from the high altar predella.

Image of St Nicholas from
the Mannerist high altar
(early 17th century).

Page 308:
The late-Gothic western portal,
decorated in relief.

Page 309:
An expressive, late-Gothic
Crucifix from the rood-arch.

INRI

In the year 2004, a place combining the beauty of nature and human ingenuity was inscribed on the World Heritage List. Moreover, the place also connects the two neighbouring nations: Poles and Germans. Of symbolic significance was the opening of the Double Bridge on 24th October 2003, as it physically put an end to the 1945 division of the park known by its Lusatian name: Park Mużakowski – The Muskauer Park. At the opening, the minister of culture of the Republic of Poland, Waldemar Dąbrowski, said: *"The Park, being a work of highest European culture, great material culture of Prussia, was torn in the Soviet zone. It would be hard to find a more symbolic place, bitterly calling to mind the tragic memory of what happened to Europe in mid-20th century. This wound has been healing for 15 years. Today, the gash between the two banks of the Neisse has finally closed, and the significance of this fact simply cannot be overestimated. I believe we have a reason for true German and Polish satisfaction. We have saved what was torn apart: what was a silent, helpless victim of history. The reconstruction of the Double Bridge on the Neisse begins the process of connecting and assimilation of this place in our individual and collective memory. The memory of the place that combines invention and creativity of the human mind, the most beautiful traditions of European culture with the tragic history of the 20th century. The process of uniting Europe acquires here a deeper if not perceptible cultural meaning."*

The vast landscape park complex covering over 700 hectares spreads on both the sides of the border Lusatian Neisse River. Majority of the park lies within the territory of the Republic of Poland. Until recently, however, the knowledge that one of Europe's most consummate works of the art of landscape management exists close at hand was absent even from the minds of residents of the nearby Łęknica and Bad Muskau. The reason for the above was far-going devastation of the park that, devoid of proper nursing, had turned into thick woods. Moreover, for many years these woods were almost inaccessible due to the "border of friendship" between Polish People's Republic and East Germany bisecting it. The restitution of the proper shape of the park and its due position in civil consciousness is owed to a group of enthusiasts who embarked on a variety of activities aimed at that already at the end of 1980s. In 1988, specialists from the Ośrodek Ochrony Zabytkowego Krajobrazu (Centre for the Preservation of Historic Landscape) performed an initial reconnaissance into the condition of the former park on the Polish side and examined its potential restitution. Of major importance was the fact that the Centre assumed the park that was formerly property of State Forests and Agricultural Property Agency of the State Treasury. To ensure appropriate protection of the Cultural Reserve established here, appropriate regulations were entered into the spatial management plan of Łęknica in 1995. The efforts aimed at legal protection of the park's future were crowned with inscription of its area (altogether 534 hectares) into the Heritage Register.

The first, highly spontaneous practical steps were taken by Polish and German preservation experts from Warsaw, Bad Muskau, Cottbus, and Berlin. They won the support of state authorities, which found its expression in 1990 in the appeal of Hans Dietrich Genscher, Germany's minister of foreign affairs, for joint restitution of the park. Of symbolic significance was the reconstruction of the Pückler Stone (1902) situated atop a hill and commemorating the founder of the park. Further work was preceded by historical research, recording of the present condition, drawing of maps, archaeological investigations of the destroyed park structures, and phytosociological studies. Their result served as basis for the detailed restoration plans. Since 1993, the park has gradually continued to return to its former beauty. Polish and German youth greatly contributed to this within the Work and Education Across Borders programme.

Obviously, complete restoration of the site was possible only thanks to international cooperation as the park is stretched on both sides of state border. It was initiated in 1989 by an agreement with the Institute for Protection of Cultural Monuments in Berlin. New potential opened when the Stiftung Fürst Pückler – Park Bad Muskau was established in Saxony in 1993. The goal of the foundation is to revive and maintain the historical park. Thanks to the foundation, Poles have gained access to the basic sources kept in German archives. Of important role are also direct contacts between specialists from the two countries that have since 1997 continued in the form of regular meetings.

Parallel to the revival, the campaign raising the awareness of the importance of the landscape park complex continued both among local community and in broader circles in Poland and abroad. Since 1994, Muskauer Park Festivities have been held regularly. The authorities of Łęknica perceive the historical park an opportunity to attract throngs of tourists to the town that has so far been famous for its gigantic flea market. Yet even the furthest reaching educational and promotional activity could not have brought such results as the inscription of Park Mużakowski – The Muskauer Park on the UNESCO World Heritage List did. The idea was embarked on in 1998, when Poles and Germans together began the preparation of appropriate documentation. For formal reasons, the odds on success seemed thin as Poland presented to UNESCO a proposal of listing a single site while

Prince Hermann von Pückler's Romantic Vision

Germany, being a federation, put forth a number of proposals on behalf of individual Lands. This taken into account, the candidate of Saxony: the Elbe Valley with Dresden, became a serious competitor for Mużaków. Another barrier was UNESCO's instruction to limit the number of European sites (as they are well represented in the List) for the benefit of Africa and other continents. And although it may seem a paradox, it was this very guideline that helped the success of the Polish-German application. With the principle of priority awarded to cross-border applications, one of the major obstacles in inscribing African sites was in most cases the requirement to have them presented by neighbouring states. Moreover, the principle applied to the same degree to all states of the world, which allowed for inscription of both the Park Mużakowski – The Muskauer Park (as a cross-border site) and the Elbe Valley.

To understand the significance of the Park Mużakowski – The Muskauer Park, it is good to be acquainted with its history. It was created by Prince Hermann Ludwig Heinrich von Pückler, a peculiar aristocrat considered an eccentric by many and the author of the literary work entitled Briefe eines Verstorbenen (published in English as: The travels of a German prince in England) that outraged his contemporaries and of a highly praised treatise on gardening. The prince began his great work in 1815 by proclaiming an open letter to the citizens of the town of Muskau, in which he announced the establishment of a great park. This entailed measures that were hardly beneficial for the local populace: ban on construction on right-bank Neisse, and even demolishing the village of Gobelin situated there. The prince planned to build a Romanticist park derived from the tradition of the sentimental, 18th-century, English garden in his estate. The principle followed in such landscaping projects was the lack of regularity, merging into the landscape, and the blurring of the border between the park and its surrounding. The designer developed the space of the park as if shaped by nature itself, while it was the human mind that subjected it to far-reaching transformations strictly subjugated to the master vision. Its execution was preceded by drafting and painting designs of individual vistas that were to unfold before the eyes of guests walking in the park. The landscape was complemented by a number of structures representing various historical styles – seemingly originating from earlier periods: gloriettes, artificial ruins, bridges, stone benches, stones with inscriptions, and imitation tombs. Following Pückler's wish, much of the park's architecture was drafted by Friedrich Schinkel himself. Two residences – the Old Castle and the New Castle – found themselves within the perimeter of the Mużaków landscape park.

The Prince never completed the garden of his dreams. In 1845, due to financial constraints he was forced to sell the estate. Three years later, it became property of a Dutch prince, Friedrich, who continued the work of his predecessor. In the years 1858–1866, an arboretum gathering a variety of tree and plant species (over 80,000 specimens brought from all over Germany and Petersburg) was established on 54 hectares. Later owners not as interested in the park, and in 1931 protection was extended over a part (240 hectares) of it. The second world war and the decades of post-war neglect brought about the obliteration of the heritage of past generations. Luckily today – thanks to the vast effort of numerous people on both banks of the Lusatian Neisse – the park, whose size and perfection dazzle most of similar Romanticist sites, can be marvelled at in its full splendour.

Fragment of an old bridge on the Lusatian Neisse that used to be the border pass between Germany and Poland.

◁

Lusatian Neisse, the border river between Poland and Germany, bisects also the park.

The Polish part of the park commands a
beautiful view of the Old and New Castles.

In the 19th century, Prince Pückler-Muskau established a park in the English style that has remained to this day as the largest site of this type in Europe.

FÜRST PÜCKLER
✳ 30. OCT. 1785 † 4. FEBR. 1871

The landscape is complemented by a number of structures representing various historical styles: gloriettes, artificial ruins, bridges, stone benches, stones with inscriptions, and imitation tombs.

Head of the road bridge.

Page 321:
The ancient oaks remember times much
before the establishment of the park...

The old cemetery today known as the
mausoleum was reconstructed by Polish
and German youth. Since 2001 its
4-metre-high cross made by the artisans
from the Jeleniogórska Valley is visible
from afar.

The Muskauer Park – Park Mużakowski
is the world's only two-state landscape park.

Page 324:
The wild and romantic path of Sarah leads
do the mysterious ravine. Its name comes
from Sarah Austin, the English translator of
Pückler's *The travels of a German prince in
England*.

The few centuries' old Oak of Odin (god of war in Norse mythology).

Jezioro Dębów (Oaken Lake) lies on the German side.

In visiting different countries and regions of the world, we are attracted to ancient works of architecture, sometimes enormous and spectacular, sometimes small and modest, and yet awe-inspiring to their age. Oftentimes, though, we encounter more recent monuments of architecture created in the 19th and 20th centuries. Many ignore them or they pay no attention to them at all. Is that the right thing to do? Most definitely not. Also such monuments of architecture deserve our attention and interest. Those who have reservations about the achievements of contemporary architecture should take into account the decision taken on July, 13, 2006 by the UNESCO Committee according to which the World Heritage List is enriched by the addition of a building which is less than a hundred years old – the People's Hall in Wrocław. The UNESCO Committee decision was inspired by the following factors:

"The Centennial Hall of Wroclaw is a creative and innovative example in the development of construction technology in large reinforced concrete structures. The Centennial Hall occupies a key position in the evolution of methods of reinforcement in architecture, and one of the climax points in the history of the use of metal in structural consolidation.

The Centennial Hall is a pioneering work of modern engineering and architecture, which exhibits an important interchange of influences in the early 20th century, becoming a key reference in the later development of reinforced concrete structures.

As part of the exhibition grounds of Wrocław, the Centennial Hall is an outstanding example of modern recreational architecture that served a variety of purposes, ranging from conferences and exhibitions to concerts, theatre and opera."

The beginning of the 20th c. was an exceptional period in many respects. It seemed that the hegemony of the European superpowers in global politics would never be broken. The Old Continent was in the throngs of the ancien régime. Power was in the hands of kings and emperors. Despite some turmoil and dramatic crises, the balance between the superpowers – Great Britain, France, Austria, Prussia and Russia – remained unchanged since 1815, when diplomats gathered in Vienna had drafted new principles on which the European politics were to be based after the turmoil caused by emperor Napoleon I.

Grand balls, ladies in splendid attire, distinguished gentlemen in uniforms and tailcoats gathered at courts and in financial circles, and in the bohemian world, uncurbed joys of a life not limited by any conventions – this is the image that the general public has of the turn of the centuries. But the charms of the fin de siècle should not make us overlook the social and political tensions which finally led to the Great War and the Bolshevik Revolution. In the dawn of those tragic events, Europe witnessed a surge in the nationalist tendencies. All nations, great and small, argued their own greatness. The ambitions of the English, the French, the German and the Russian led to the increased desire for confrontation, while the smaller nations voiced their just claims to independence more and more loudly. It was in this atmosphere that monuments were being created all over Europe in order to prove the superiority of one superpower over another or the rights to independence of nations suffering under imposed foreign power. Most often they were sculpted monuments of different kinds: leaders on horseback, poets standing pensive or inspired, great explorers and scholars in bust. But also monuments of architecture were erected to commemorate events past.

In the German Empire, memory was carefully cultivated of one of the largest, bloodiest and most significant battles in the history of Europe – the encounter between Napoleon I's army and the anti-Napoleon coalition outside Leipzig in 1813. The army of the French Emperor, assisted by the Polish troops commanded by Prince Józef Poniatowski were squarely defeated. In preparation for the centenary of the event, an enormous construction was designed and erected in Leipzig, which towers over the city to this day. Also other towns of the Reich prepared for the approaching centenary of the battle. In Wrocław, a decision on organising the Centennial Exhibition was taken as early as in 1907. For the purpose, grounds adjacent to the Szczytnicki Park, in the vicinity of the present Zoological Garden and the horserace track, were assigned. The celebrations were to centre around a large exhibition hall, for which Max Berg's daring design was selected from among 43 projects. In June 1911, the official permit was issued for the construction and the monument was completed by December 1912. The smaller pavilions around the hall and its surroundings were designed by Hans Poelzig.

At the time, Wrocław could boast the world's largest reinforced-concrete building, with the maximum width of 95 m, the height of 42 m, and the roof diameter of 67 m. The building could accommodate up to 10,000 people. As if this were not sufficient, inside, the world's largest organ was installed with 222 registers and 16,706 pipes, manufactured by the Wilhelm Sauer company at Frankfurt an der Oder. Unfortunately, the organ was disassembled in 1946, and the parts remaining were used among others for the construction of the organ presently installed in the Wrocław cathedral.

The monumental character of the construction was expressed by the bas-relief placed over the gateway, which has not been preserved to our day. The relief represented Archangel Michael fighting the dragon, as a symbol of the victory achieved a hundred years earlier over the much-despised Napoleon. The visitors to the jubilee exhibition in 1913 could also read an excerpt from a proclamation issued by Emperor Frederick William III on March 17, 1813: *"He who feels for his country does not think of himself. Follow the example of your ancestors, be*

The Centennial Hall (The People's Hall) – a useful monument

worthy of them and remindful of your followers".

After the end of WWI, the hall served for large gatherings, and also accommodated concerts and theatre performances. However, the influence of a new, menacing ideology began to be felt here, too. On April 18, 1932, the hall was home to Adolf Hitler's election meeting. In 1934, newspapers wrote: *„As in the construction concept of the hall, which is clearly manifested in four bent pillars and a dome resting on them, so the four main pillars of the new German people: duty, freedom, brotherhood and unity, should be represented by monumental painting and sculpture".*

Also after WWII, which the hall luckily survived, attempts were made to involve it in the propaganda of the new system, this time – communism. The hall was renamed from Centennial Hall to People's Hall. Between August 25 and 28, 1948, the hall witnessed the World Congress of Intellectuals in Defence of Peace, which strove to convince the world of the (oxymoronic) necessity of the struggle for peace under the auspices of the Soviet Union. The Regained Territories Exhibition, in turn, was meant as a testimony to the economic developments in the areas newly assigned to Poland by the Yalta Conference decisions. The event is commemorated by a 300-feet steel steeple placed in front of the main entrance. It was claimed to be the „triumph of both Polish technology and inventiveness, and of hard work, the symbol of our optimism".

Luckily, the Wrocław inhabitants associate the hall mostly with various sports and entertainment events. Between the 1970's and 1995, the concert hall housed the Gigant cinema, which could seat up to 4,000 spectators. The hall also witnesed an event of the highest rank – the visit of Pope John Paul II, who partcipated in an ecumenical meeting on May 3, 1997 on the occasion of the International Eucharistic Congress. In recent years, the hall has been modernised and it has become a major attraction for music lovers, who are lured by large-scale, impressive theatre performances.

Times have changed and so has the role of the building, but the monumental hall is still a tribute to the genius of Max Berg, who was among those who laid foundations for contemporary architecture. The construction of the impressive Wrocław landmark was made possible thanks to the use of a new technology of reinforced concrete. At present, the construction industry could not do without it, but at the turn of the 20th c. the technology was a novelty and its value was not fully known. Most importantly, experiments involving reinforced concrete allowed erecting constructions based on large-span arches, and also the development of skeleton constructions. Numerous architects have used the new material to implement projects remindful of the past styles – for instance before WWI, the principles of monumental classicism were often evoked. Berg went in a different direction. Faithful to the principle of "honesty to the material", he left the raw surface of the reinforced concrete without "refining" it or covering with a surface of stone or plaster. Moreover, the architect retained the pure, daring construction of intersecting arches, which support rings forming the step-pyramid shape of the building. The architect has fully used the natural beauty of the logical, monumental structure, which does not need to be complete by elements evoking historical architectural styles and ornaments. The Centennial Hall evokes the spirit of the past in a different manner: it has been constructed on the plan of a circle combined with a quadrifolium, which is encountered in numerous ancient churches. The central plan used to be considered to be the most perfect, and as such it was often used in sacral buildings. Max Berg clearly made a conscious allusion to the monumental constructions of the type, and more particularly to Rome's Pantheon and the Hagia Sophia in Constantinople (presently, Istanbul). In this manner, he has for ever entered the great tradition of European architecture.

The Centennial Hall dome – an important step in the development of reinforced concrete technology.

The monumental construction towering above a pond situated in the nearby park.

The book was published
on the initiative
of Biały Kruk
Publishing House

Biały Kruk Sp. z o.o.
ul. Szwedzka 38
PL 30-324 Kraków
Tel./Fax: + 48 12/260 32 40
              260 32 90
              260 34 50
e-mail: biuro@bialykruk.pl
www.bialykruk.pl

2nd edition - complemented
Cracow 2007
ISBN 978-83-60292-32-9